THE
PERFECT
MORTGAGE

THE
PERFECT
MORTGAGE

YOUR KEY TO CUTTING THE COST OF HOME OWNERSHIP

ALAN SILVERSTEIN

Stoddart

First published in 1989 by
Stoddart Publishing Co. Limited
34 Lesmill Road
Toronto, Canada
M3B 2T6

CANADIAN CATALOGUING IN PUBLICATION DATA

Silverstein, Alan, 1951-
    The perfect mortgage

ISBN 0-7737-5276-5

1. Mortgage loans – Canada 2. Mortgages – Canada
I. Title

HG2040.5.C3S54 1989   332.7′2′0971   C89-093436-3

Cover Design: Brant Cowie/ArtPlus Limited
Printed in Canada

Mary bought a little house
And booked a mortgage too,
All she compared were interest rates
Just like most borrowers do.

She turned her back on other points,
Thinking mortgages were all the same.
"Why shop for debt? That's crazy!
What do I have to gain?"

When Mary sold that little house
Imagine her surprise:
The $3,000 prepayment charge
Brought tears to her eyes.

"Next time I'll shop for features
That are the best for me
And use The Perfect Mortgage
To borrow, worry-free."

Contents

Acknowledgments

Special words of thanks to my two superb secretaries, Donna Boisselle and Connie Romanyshyn. Their loyalty, care and dedication to the day-to-day details of my law practice is so greatly appreciated.

Thank you to the staff at Stoddart Publishing for their support of *The Perfect Mortgage* concept. Their commitment to providing the best information on real estate, home buying and mortgage financing is unsurpassed in Canada.

The most important and sincere thank you belongs to my family, my loving wife, Hannah, and my two wonderful sons, Elliott and Darryl. No words can adequately express the encouragement, support and understanding they have given me. To Hannah, Elliott and Darryl I dedicate this book for they, more than anyone, are responsible for its becoming a reality.

1
The Perfect Mortgage

Does it exist?

Without a doubt, the best mortgage is no mortgage! While that's especially true in Canada, where mortgage interest generally can't be written off against other income, most people still need a mortgage when buying a house. After all, there are only two ways to pay for that house—with your money or somebody else's money. The less cash you have, the more you have to borrow. There's no third alternative.

What is the first thing most people think about when looking for a mortgage? The interest rate. And that makes sense, because no one wants to pay more for a mortgage than necessary. But interest rates should only be the first point to consider when shopping for a mortgage, never the last (or sole) feature.

Today there is very little variation in interest rates amongst the major lenders. Compare the interest rates published weekly in many newspapers, and you'll be surprised at how similar they really are. Unless the rates have changed and individual lenders have not yet followed suit, most lenders charge the identical rate of interest for any given term (six months to five years).

If rates are all the same, is there more to a mortgage than interest rates? *Yes, yes, yes!* Not all mortgages are created equal. Mortgage packages vary significantly from lender to lender, with no two lenders offering identical packages of features and options. With no real difference in rates, these other distinguishing factors must be carefully considered when booking a mortgage loan. The similarity of interest rates is surpassed only by the diversity of the features in these mortgage packages.

More and more new products are available to residential mortgage borrowers than ever before. With so much variety to choose from, Canadians find the selection process increasingly confusing and difficult. Which features are good and which ones are not? Which options will truly save borrowers money, and which ones benefit lenders? While a certain idea may not be too helpful today, remember that it could be important (and save considerable money) in the not-too-distant future.

Understandably, every lender promotes its mortgage package as "the best for the borrower." Yet with the large amounts of money involved today, borrowers can't afford to make a mistake, or they may later become disenchanted with what the mortgage offers. Small wonder Canadian mortgage borrowers are in a quandary. What should they do? These four things:

- Look for a mortgage that offers the most liberalized pre-payment privileges available.
- Look for options and features that provide the maximum in flexibility, whether renewing the loan or selling the house.
- Look for a mortgage that offers the lowest possible interest costs, with the fewest hidden charges.
- Look for a lender whose package best reflects your unique circumstances.

In other words, Canadian mortgage borrowers must become educated consumers, and then diligently shop for those features which make up the perfect mortgage. If you're going to play the game, you've got to know the rules.

BE A SMART SHOPPER

No lender today offers the perfect mortgage. But just because the perfect mortgage doesn't exist, doesn't mean it can't exist. In fact, *every feature* making up the perfect mortgage described in this book is available today from some major institutional lender. Unfortunately, no one lender has had the vision or courage to combine the best features into the perfect mortgage.

But knowing the rules of the mortgage game just isn't enough. Residential borrowers also need a *strategy* when shopping for a mortgage. First, carefully analyze which features of the perfect mortgage are most appealing and important. Since no lender offers everything you are looking for, draw up a "needs and wants" list. Features that you absolutely must have are "needs," while those you would like to include are "wants." List them in order of priority, creating your own personalized ranking system. The mortgage arranged should provide the greatest number of perfect mortgage features, satisfying all of your needs and as many of your wants as possible.

Then carefully and prudently shop the market looking for that mortgage, asking lenders a multitude of questions about what their packages include. Remember, there is more—much more—to a mortgage than its rate. When inquiring whether a lender offers a particular feature, borrowers will soon learn the answer usually is that some do and some don't—it depends on the individual lender. All the more reason why it's necessary to diligently shop for the best possible terms.

Once you find a lender that offers the features you find most desirable, *make 100% sure those features will appear right in the mortgage that you sign*. Being told it's the policy of the lender to offer these options is not enough. Policy can change overnight with a directive from head office. A feature that is written into the mortgage is unalterable.

Negotiating a mortgage loan is somewhat different from buying a car or a house. There, the overall package is the sum total of the individual items included or excluded. Negotiating a mortgage means discovering which of the perfect mortgage options a particular lender provides. If a certain feature is not available as part of that lender's package, little can be done to have it included. Borrowers must continue their search until they find a lender that provides what they are looking for.

Shopping for a mortgage—that's a strange-sounding expression. Usually we only consider shopping for assets; why would anyone ever want to shop for debt? What we forget, especially with mortgages, is how the features and options associated with that debt differ from lender to lender. The only way to book a mortgage with the best possible terms, *and then to get rid of that debt as quickly and cheaply as possible*, is to carefully shop for it. Otherwise, the hidden charges and clauses could wreak financial havoc for borrowers. Prudent residential borrowers will shop for mortgage money as thoroughly and diligently as they shop for an asset such as a house, and book a mortgage that comes as close to the perfect mortgage as possible. The alternative is just too risky.

An important part of this mortgage strategy for home buyers is the "preapproved" mortgage (discussed in Chapter 2), where the mortgage is arranged before the house is even bought. But even preapproved mortgages have their drawbacks. Still, purchasers should never leave the question of arranging a mortgage to the very end, considering it for the first time once an Agreement of Purchase and Sale has been signed. That is even more dangerous.

Shopping for the perfect mortgage does not apply only to buyers arranging a mortgage to finance a purchase. In recent years, changing lenders when a mortgage matures to take advantage of the perfect mortgage features has become easier and cheaper than ever. With an increasing number of shorter-term mortgages being arranged, there are more and more opportunities for current homeowners to switch lenders all the time. This strategy of actively seeking the most desirable mortgage features is equally important for anyone booking a mortgage for a home purchase, or whose mortgage is coming up for renewal.

Summarized at the end of each chapter is a shopping list of questions to ask when examining different lenders' packages. The information in the chapter is the meat on the bones, the answers to seek when asking the questions. Several chapters at the end of *The Perfect Mortgage* explore other important topics:

- How to structure a larger-than-average loan;
- The strengths and weaknesses of short-term and long-term mortgages;
- The options available on mortgage maturity;
- The home equity loan.

Overall, *The Perfect Mortgage* provides an objective overview of the residential Canadian mortgage market today. Its goal is simple—to help turn "Home Sweet Home" into a "Loan Free Home"!

Armed with this essential information about rules and strategies, borrowers can confidently negotiate the mortgage package that is best for them. Instead of going cap-in-hand for a mortgage, borrowers can stand shoulder-to-shoulder with the lender. If they have done their homework, the question borrowers face is no longer whether they will get a mortgage loan; instead, it is who will grant it, and on what terms. Instead of negotiating from a position of weakness, borrowers will negotiate from strength.

Enough of the preliminaries. It's time to start revealing the best-kept secret in Canada, the mystery of the perfect mortgage.

2
Preapproved Mortgages

They can be beneficial, but dangerous too

When buying a house years ago, most people like Ward and June gave very little thought to the mortgage until the end, almost as if it were an afterthought. Once the offer was signed, conditional on arranging a mortgage within a short period of time, Ward and June would scurry about for financing. The first mortgage package presented, whatever the terms, was usually accepted, since they lacked the luxury of time to shop carefully. Waiting for word whether a mortgage would be granted caused considerable anxiety for buyers. And if they couldn't arrange the financing in time, Ward and June would lose the house.

But it wasn't only home buyers who were on pins and needles. Homeowners like Fred and Wilma who wanted to refinance an existing loan also faced uncertainty awaiting final approval of their application. If only these home buyers and owners could have known in advance that they qualified for a mortgage. Not only would it have reduced or eliminated their aggravation, it would have allowed them to confidently shop for the mortgage with the best possible terms for them—the perfect mortgage.

How times have changed! Every major institutional lender today claims to have "a preapproved mortgage just for you." While the term "preapproved" (or as it is sometimes dubbed— "prearranged") mortgage is a paradox, it means purchasers/borrowers like Ward and June have the security of receiving preliminary approval for a mortgage even *before* buying a house. They confidently know how much they can afford to borrow and therefore how much they can afford to buy (based on their down payment). This eliminates the need for an offer "conditional on financing," making it more attractive to their seller. Current owners like Fred and Wilma also can be preapproved for a refinancing well before their mortgage matures. Usually the turnaround time for a decision, from application to approval, is quite short—48 to 72 hours.

5

Preapproved mortgages are a new idea, a marketing tool reflecting the recent heightened competition amongst financial institutions for new mortgage business. No lenders charge for their preapproved mortgages. Some lenders give qualifying applicants a letter of approval or wallet-sized certificate, just like a credit card, stating the maximum mortgage amount available and what the payments will be! Usually one condition is attached to the preapproval—that the lender receive a satisfactory appraisal of the property once it is purchased. But even when borrowers are preapproved for a mortgage, there's still no obligation to deal with that lender. There is nothing to stop borrowers preapproved by one lender from booking their mortgage elsewhere if they can get a better deal.

When there is upward pressure on interest rates, a preapproved mortgage preserves a previously committed, lower rate of interest. Unfortunately, preapproved mortgages have very short rate-guarantee periods. Depending on the state of the market and the lender, it could be valid for anywhere from 30 to 90 days. To keep the rate, borrowers must complete their refinancing during that time or purchasers must find a house, sign a contract and close the purchase. Otherwise, the benefit of the committed rate is gone, and the borrower must reapply all over again. Therefore, when shopping for a preapproved mortgage, ask the lender how long the rate is guaranteed. And see if the commitment period runs from the date of the application, or the date of the approval—another important consideration when rates are on the rise.

DON'T TAKE IT TOO EASY WITH YOUR PREAPPROVED MORTGAGE

Preapproved mortgages are one of the most important and innovative features in mortgage financing in recent years. Yet despite their apparent attractiveness, to the surprise of many people, preapproved mortgages can be dangerous. How? Because they are too convenient, and make life too easy and simple for most borrowers. Unless they are careful, borrowers could fall into an unsuspected and costly trap with a preapproved mortgage. Even with a preapproved mortgage it's necessary for borrowers to look before they leap, and to shop before they sign.

David and Pat are thinking of buying a house. Anxious to

know how much they can afford to borrow, they applied to Amortization Trust, where they do all their banking, for a preapproved mortgage. In 48 hours they had a clear idea how much they could afford to borrow. Coupled with their down payment, David and Pat knew the approximate price they could afford to pay for a house. Then, assured the financing was available, David and Pat went into the marketplace, found a house, and signed an Offer to Purchase. They didn't have to make the offer conditional on arranging financing—why should they? They had a preapproved mortgage!

A common scenario? Of course. But what is wrong with what David and Pat did? Just as most people would do, they applied for a preapproved mortgage with a lender—but just *one* lender. They did no mortgage shopping before applying to Amortization Trust. And after receiving confirmation of how much they could borrow, David and Pat stopped even thinking about shopping further. Since they had been preapproved, why look elsewhere? While David and Pat still could have sought another preapproved mortgage elsewhere, how likely was that? Having been preapproved by Amortization Trust, they somehow felt obligated to deal just with it. Practically speaking, once they were preapproved, the search for a mortgage was over.

Yet this convenience is what makes the preapproved mortgage so dangerous. Because it was so easy to arrange, David and Pat never thoroughly compared different lenders' money-saving options and features. They never analyzed which features of the perfect mortgage were most appealing and important. They never examined the prepayment privilege offered by lenders other than Amortization Trust. Instead of just being convenient, the preapproved mortgage was too convenient! Granted, David and Pat now had a mortgage. But how would they really know if it was the most appropriate overall package for them unless they considered what other lenders offered?

What should David and Pat have done? Followed this three-step program:

1) Informally prequalify themselves for a mortgage. David and Pat should first answer exactly the same questions as a lender will consider, *before* contacting a lender. This way they will know at the outset the approximate size of mortgage they qualify for, plus how expensive a home they can buy.

2) Shop for a lender offering mortgage features they like. Armed with those preliminary answers, David and Pat would diligently look for lenders who offer the greatest number of the perfect mortgage features as possible.

3) Get formally preapproved for a mortgage with a lender that has the features they want. Once they have found several lenders whose packages fit the bill, then, and only then, would David and Pat actually apply for a preapproved mortgage. If they followed the process properly, David and Pat should be told what they already know—how much they can afford to borrow, and how much they can afford to buy.

This three-stage approach enables David and Pat to negotiate the best possible mortgage deal with the best overall terms, *and know that when they book it.*

PLAY THE ROLE OF THE LENDER

What do lenders consider in deciding whether to grant a mortgage? What do lenders consider in issuing a preapproved mortgage? What should you consider in prequalifying yourself for a mortgage? Both the property and the borrower.

1) The property. "Conventional" first mortgages do not exceed 75% of the lesser of a) the sale price and b) the appraised value of the property. This "loan to value" ratio requires that for conventional first mortgages, the borrower's equity in the property be at least 25% of its appraised value. For a property appraised at $200,000, the maximum conventional first mortgage will be 75% of that figure, or $150,000. The remaining 25% or $50,000 must come from the borrower's own resources.

Calculating how large a conventional mortgage will satisfy the property requirement is very simple. Assuming the purchase price is the appraised value, just multiply the amount of money available as a down payment by three. For example, a $30,000 down payment will permit a conventional mortgage of $90,000. If the mortgage needed to buy the home is no larger than this, you've passed the property-value test.

But Henry and Sue Ellen do not have enough money to pay 25% of the purchase price on closing. This doesn't mean they can't buy a house! Since they need a mortgage for more than 75% of the appraised value (known in the industry as a "high ratio" loan), Henry and Sue Ellen have two options. Either they must a) arrange a second mortgage for that portion of the loan that exceeds 75% of the appraised value or b) arrange one large mortgage with "mortgage payment insurance" on the entire loan (and not just the portion exceeding 75% of the appraised value). This mortgage payment insurance, which protects the lender if the borrower defaults, is available through CMHC (Canada Mortgage and Housing Corporation, a government agency) or MICC (the Mortgage Insurance Company of Canada, a private insurer). Either way there will be extra costs in arranging the financing. And whether it's two smaller mortgages or one big mortgage, Henry and Sue Ellen must have good incomes to compensate for the smaller-than-normal down payment. (More information on these two options appears in Chapter 18.)

2) The borrower, and his/her/their ability to repay the loan. Lenders want to be sure borrowers like Henry and Sue Ellen have gross annual incomes large enough and sufficiently stable to carry the mortgage. The combined gross annual incomes of both spouses are usually considered if both have solid jobs with a strong likelihood of continued employment.

As on any loan application, mortgage lenders want extensive information about the borrower and his/her/their financial resources. This includes a detailed personal net-worth statement of assets and liabilities, sources of income, employment particulars verified by a letter from an employer or an income tax return, and credit references. Usually this is followed by a credit check. Especially on purchases an "equity" letter from the buyer's bank may be necessary, indicating that sufficient money is available to pay the balance of the purchase price on closing.

In looking at the borrowers, the generally accepted rule is that no more than 30% of their gross annual incomes be applied to the principal, interest and taxes (and maintenance where the security is a condominium unit). This is the GDS ratio, or Gross Debt Service ratio. Another calculation, the Total Debt Service or TDS ratio, looks at the amount of gross annual income needed to service all debts—house, car loans, personal loans and credit card loans. Depending on the lender, TDS payments should not exceed 37% to 40% of the borrowers' gross annual incomes. Most lenders adhere quite strictly to these rules.

The link between the size of a mortgage and the borrowers' gross annual incomes means the same question can be asked two different ways. How large a mortgage can be supported by their gross annual incomes? How large must their gross annual incomes be to support a certain-sized mortgage?

Henry and Sue Ellen have a combined gross annual income of $50,000. Calculating whether the cost of carrying a house will exceed 30% of their gross annual incomes is complicated. After taking 30% of $50,000, it must be allocated amongst principal, interest and taxes. This is what a lender will do when Henry and Sue Ellen formally apply for a preapproved mortgage.

But there is a much easier and quicker way for Henry and Sue Ellen to learn whether their gross annual incomes will qualify for a certain-sized mortgage. When informally prequalifying for a mortgage, all Henry and Sue Ellen must do is combine the monthly mortgage payment (principal and interest) amortized over 25 years with one-twelfth of the realty taxes (and the monthly condominium maintenance payment, if applicable). Then they multiply this figure by 40. If their gross annual incomes exceed the result, the GDS ratio has been satisfied, and they should qualify for the mortgage. Presto! By prequalifying themselves for a mortgage, Henry and Sue Ellen now know what to expect when they formally apply for a preapproved mortgage.

The formula to calculate the gross income needed to service a mortgage is:

$$\begin{matrix} \text{monthly} \\ \text{mortgage} \\ \text{payment} \\ \text{for a} \\ \text{mortgage of} \\ \$ \\ \text{at} \quad \% \end{matrix} + \begin{matrix} \text{estimated} \\ \text{monthly} \\ \text{property} \\ \text{taxes} \end{matrix} + \begin{matrix} \text{monthly} \\ \text{condominium} \\ \text{maintenance} \\ \text{payment} \\ \text{if applicable} \end{matrix} \times 40 = \begin{matrix} \text{gross} \\ \text{income} \\ \text{needed} \end{matrix}$$

How do Henry and Sue Ellen know what the monthly mortgage payment (principal and interest) amortized over

25 years will be? The chart below shows the payments per month per thousand dollars of borrowed money at different interest rates. This is the key to Henry and Sue Ellen prequalifying themselves for the mortgage.

THE PAYMENT PER MONTH PER THOUSAND DOLLARS OF BORROWED MONEY AT VARIOUS INTEREST RATES, ASSUMING A 25-YEAR AMORTIZATION

interest rate	payment	interest rate	payment
10	8.95	15	12.46
10.5	9.28	15.5	12.83
11	9.63	16	13.19
11.5	9.97	16.5	13.56
12	10.32	17	13.93
12.5	10.67	17.5	14.29
13	11.02	18	14.66
13.5	11.38	18.5	15.03
14	11.74	19	15.41
14.5	12.10	19.5	15.78
		20	16.15

Say Henry and Sue Ellen want to borrow $100,000 and current interest rates are 12%. The cost per month per thousand for that loan is $10.32, meaning the monthly payment for $100,000 will be $10.32 times 100 or approximately $1,032. According to the real estate agent, property taxes are $125 per month (the property is not a condominium). To see what the income threshold is, add $1,032 plus $125 for a total of $1,157, and multiply the result by 40 for a final total of $46,280. Since their gross annual incomes exceed this figure, Henry and Sue Ellen satisfy the GDS ratio test.

When Henry and Sue Ellen apply for a preapproved mortgage, the lender will start with their income and work backwards, employing a number of lengthy calculations to see how much money they can borrow. In seconds Henry and Sue Ellen have determined at the prequalifying stage whether their gross annual incomes are large enough to carry a certain-sized mortgage. Either way the result is the same. But there is one important distinction—by having prequalified themselves for a mortgage, Henry and Sue Ellen now can do some comparative shopping for a mortgage from a position of strength. Knowing what the ultimate answers will be, they can confidently seek the best overall mortgage package with the lender offering the greatest number of the perfect mortgage features. How refreshingly different this is from the norm!

When Shopping for the Perfect Mortgage, Ask:

1) Does the lender offer a preapproved mortgage? What conditions are attached to the loan?
2) How long is the interest rate guaranteed?
3) Does the lender employ the "usual" rules dealing with both the property and the borrower in deciding whether to grant a mortgage?

3
Some Preliminary Considerations

A basic primer in mortgages

Before considering the major distinguishing features of mortgages, it's necessary to have a basic understanding of what they are. Here are some commonly-used mortgage expressions.

Mortgage It's nothing more than a fancy form of an IOU; security for the repayment of a debt. When a loan is booked, the lender gives money to the borrower in return for the mortgage. When the loan is paid off the reverse happens—the borrower returns the money to the lender and the lender gives the borrower a "discharge" or release of the mortgage. Of course, a mortgage is much more elaborate than just an IOU. Registered against the title to the borrower's property, it provides various remedies to the lender if the borrower doesn't pay on time.

Principal The amount initially borrowed from the lender.

Interest The lender's charge to the borrower for the use of the money lent. Just as a landlord charges rent for the use of his/her/its property (an apartment), borrowers face a "rent charge" called interest when using the lender's property (his/her/its money). It is only charged on the amount of principal outstanding at any point in time. The less principal owing, the less interest payable.

Term The life of the mortgage; how long the mortgage has to run until it "matures." Mortgage terms generally are as short as six months, or as long as five years or more. When the term is up and the mortgage matures, the entire amount outstanding on the mortgage is due and payable. *Do not confuse the expression "term" with amortization; they are totally separate ideas.*

Amortization The length of time it would take to fully repay the loan, assuming there were no prepayments (early payments) and no late payments, and assuming that the same interest rate was charged at each renewal. It is little more than a calculation period, the normal amortization being 25 years. A typical mortgage with a three-year term and a 25-year amortization would have a life of three years, and payments calculated as if they would be made continuously over 25 years.

There are four components in calculating mortgages—the principal, the interest rate, the amortization and the payment. Select any three and the fourth component is calculated automatically. If a mortgage has an outstanding principal of $100,000, an interest rate of 12% per annum calculated semi-annually, not in advance (a typical Canadian mortgage, described in more detail in Chapter 5), and is amortized over 25 years, the blended monthly payment is $1,031.90. (With a blended payment, the same amount is paid each period [whether monthly, weekly, biweekly or semi-monthly] during the mortgage term. But with each payment the allocation towards principal and interest changes. Over time more money goes to principal and less to interest.)

If you keep two of the numbers constant and change the third, the fourth automatically changes. Therefore, assume the outstanding principal remains at $100,000 and the interest rate at 12% per annum. Reducing the amortization to 20 years would affect the blended monthly payment—in this case increasing it to $1,080.98. For the same mortgage, keeping the amortization at 25 years but increasing the interest rate to 12.5% results in a new monthly payment of $1,067.03.

To learn how much of a blended payment is principal and how much is interest, or how much is outstanding on a mortgage at any time, lenders and borrowers rely on a computer printout called an amortization (or AM) schedule. On page 135 is a typical AM schedule for a mortgage with an outstanding principal of $100,000, an interest rate of 12% per annum calculated semi-annually (not in advance), amortized over 25 years, and blended monthly payments of $1,031.90. This is the "standard mortgage" against which all other mortgages will be compared in this book.

As the amortization schedule indicates, mortgages are heavily "front-end loaded," with virtually all of the payments at the beginning applied against the interest. Most of the interest on the loan will be paid in its early years. Of the $12,382.80 paid the first year, over 94% of it, or $11,673.26, was interest, interest, interest! The total overall interest cost for this mortgage, also known as the cost of borrowing, over 25 years will be $209,569.28, assuming the interest rate didn't change over those 25 years.

On top of that, the original $100,000 has to be repaid as well. In other words, the cost of financing this loan is over twice the size of the original mortgage.

But that is not the whole story. Remember that in Canada interest on residential mortgages generally is not deductible against other income. Put another way, we make our mortgage payments from "after-tax" dollars, money on which income tax has already been paid. This means we have to earn a lot more money than we think, and pay a sizable portion of that in income tax, to cover the interest on our home mortgages.

Look again at the state of the mortgage after the first year, where the total payments were $12,382.80, of which $11,673.26 was interest and just $709.54 principal. If tax reform left us in the $33^1/_3\%$ tax bracket, we have to earn $17,509.89 at work the first year alone and pay $5,836.63 income tax to have the $11,673.26 to pay the interest that prunes down the principal by just $709.54!

Canadians are saying there has got to be a better way. And there is—by prepaying your mortgage. Small dollar prepayments mean big savings, especially in the early years of the mortgage. Making no attempt to prepay your mortgage is the worst thing a borrower can do. Doing nothing may mean slightly lower monthly payments, but unnecessarily higher interest costs. But to prepay your mortgage, it's absolutely essential to have the most liberal prepayment privileges available. And as we will see in Chapter 7, no two lenders offer the same prepayment privileges.

This explains why Canadians must shop carefully for a mortgage. Without the best possible mortgage features, borrowers will find themselves saddled with this albatross called a mortgage for a generation to come.

4
Interest Rate and Term

The first of many choices

When shopping for a mortgage, the first thing borrowers think about is the interest rate. More than any other factor, interest rates affect the number of purchasers entering or withdrawing from the market. As rates go up, fewer people look for houses. The reverse is true as rates decline. But most, if not all, lenders charge the same rate of interest for the same mortgage term. A random sampling of mortgage rates at different financial institutions would confirm this.

After interest rates, borrowers wonder how long a mortgage to book. Today, mortgages are readily available for terms as short as six months, and as long as five years. A handful of lenders even offer seven- and 10-year terms. Complicating matters is the fact that interest rates and mortgage terms are closely intertwined. Short-term mortgages (six months to a year) generally carry interest rates that are 1% to 1.5% lower than their long-term counterparts (five years). What a dilemma!

Why are rates the same, no matter who lends the money, and why do rates differ depending on the term of the mortgage? The answer lies in the nature of the money-lending system. Lenders are money brokers who deal in money the same way a peddler sells fruit. Just as the fruit peddler buys fruit wholesale and sells it retail, banks and trust companies "buy" money at one rate of interest. Money is borrowed from the public through term deposits, guaranteed investment certificates and savings accounts. After "marking it up" just like the fruit peddler, the financial institutions then "sell" money, lending it through mortgages at a higher rate of interest. For the fruit peddler the sale price less the cost price is the profit. For the banker, the difference in the interest rates (the "spread") is the profit.

All lending institutions use a "matching principle" when setting their mortgage rates that links mortgages (the lending vehicle) with savings deposits (the borrowing vehicle) having the same term. What is available greatly depends on how the public prefers to save its money. The more five-year money a lender has on deposit, the more five-year money that can be lent out as mortgages. Or the reverse could be the case if the public decided to place its money into short-term savings vehicles.

What factors influence interest rates? Short-term mortgage rates closely parallel changes in the Bank of Canada rate, which is based on the rate for 91-day Government of Canada Treasury Bills set every Thursday. In turn, it depends on a number of factors such as the strength of the Canadian dollar in international money markets, the level of economic growth and inflation.

Long-term mortgage rates reflect the rates for alternative long-term investment vehicles—guaranteed investment certificates and bonds—as well as lenders' inflationary expectations. But a shift in long-term savings account rates can also affect the amount of money deposited into short-term savings vehicles, and therefore the amount of money available for short-term mortgages. And the same is also true in reverse, when short-term deposit rates change.

To be competitive in this environment, no institutional lender can afford to charge rates significantly different than other lenders. Whenever there is a major change in the cost of obtaining money, it may take a week or two or three for all the major financial institutions to follow suit. But then, once again, mortgage interest rates will be similar, if not identical, for loans with identical terms. Private mortgage lenders tend simply to adopt the interest rates established by "the big boys."

Predicting where interest rates will be in the future means playing the biggest legal crap game in town. The same is true in deciding whether to book a short-term mortgage (one year or less), go long-term (five years or more) or play it conservative and select something in between. Since important safeguards must be included regardless which option is chosen, that specific question will be considered later in this book, after examining some of the other factors that go into the perfect mortgage. In the meantime, keep the following ideas in mind when considering a mortgage term and an interest rate. And remember they apply equally when arranging a new mortgage to finance a purchase, or if you are refinancing your mortgage when it matures.

There is no simple right or wrong answer when deciding which mortgage term and (indirectly) which interest rate to select. Good arguments can be made for both types of loans. The first point borrowers should consider is their own personal situation, and their own personal makeup.

Borrowers generally pay a higher rate of interest for long-term mortgages, a "premium" for security. But this protection against wildly gyrating interest rates is the key attraction of long-term mortgages. Consider the $100,000, five-year, 12% mortgage William arranged recently, described on page 135. Rick, on the other hand, chose a six-month mortgage at an interest rate of 10.5%. William is sheltered from the interest-rate market for the next five years, no matter how erratic it might be. Because he put the issue to bed for the next five years, William can sleep each night immune to changes in the Bank of Canada rate and bond prices. The higher price tag William pays each year during the entire mortgage term—an additional 1.5% in interest—really is a form of insurance to obtain the stability of a long-term commitment. The occasional lender will even offer "super-long-term" mortgages—seven and 10 years—at even higher interest rates (a minimum of 0.5% over the five-year rate). Long-term mortgages with a low, fixed interest rate are still the first choice of Canadians.

Rick now faces the volatility and instability of the interest-rate merry-go-round much more frequently, perhaps once or twice a year. But because Rick is prepared to stomach the interest-rate market more often, he can benefit from the greatest advantage of the short-term mortgage—the lower interest rate it bears. The 10.5% rate means his monthly payment is $928.33 compared with William's $1,031.90. A significant savings, indeed.

Don't interpret this as a blanket endorsement for short-term mortgages. Other factors must be considered in selecting a mortgage term, such as how long you expect to stay in the home. If it's only three to four years, choose a mortgage term that reflects your anticipated period of ownership. And if in doubt, round that number down, not up. A five-year mortgage means paying more each month for a benefit you'll never use. And if the house is sold before the mortgage matures, you may have to pay a sizable prepayment penalty to cancel the loan.

Borrowers also generally pay a higher rate of interest for short-term mortgages that are "fully open," allowing any amount to be prepaid whenever the borrower wants and without any penalty (examined in greater detail in Chapter 8). Arthur and Jane pay a "premium" for flexibility here, since the rate on a six-month, fully open mortgage is often set 0.5% higher than that for a six-month, fully closed mortgage.

A new feature in the marketplace—the "portable mortgage"—could have a significant impact in resolving the short-term/long-term dilemma. Portable mortgages can be taken from one property to another on a sale of the property (they are examined in greater detail in Chapter 15). With a portable mortgage, borrowers could easily select a long-term mortgage, knowing there will be no prepayment penalty if they sell their home before the mortgage matures. In many ways portability tilts the scale in favour of the long-term mortgage and makes it viable.

The development of the short-term mortgage has an interesting background. As a response to the extremely high interest rates of the day, in the early 1980s institutional lenders introduced variable-rate mortgages (VRMs). In contrast to fixed-rate mortgages, the interest rate could be adjusted as frequently as every month, based on changes in the inflation rate and the cost of borrowing. While VRMs passed on the risk of fluctuating interest rates directly to borrowers, the trade-off was a fully open loan, one that the borrower could pay off at any time.

As the interest rate charged was adjusted during the term of the mortgage, VRMs helped guarantee the interest "spread" that lenders need to operate. VRMs also made it easy for lenders to properly match the inflow of savings funds with mortgage money being lent out during one of the most volatile periods in our economic history.

As interest rates began to fall and then stabilize around the 12% mark, the public began to turn its back on VRMs. Circumstances were different now. Who wanted a mortgage where the rate could be increased each month? VRMs offered absolutely no stability to borrowers. But lenders had come to enjoy the ease of matching funds using VRMs. Something similar to a VRM was needed that would recapture the public's imagination for the product.

The result: the six-month, fully open mortgage. In reality it is nothing more than a VRM where the interest rate is guaranteed for the entire six-month term, regardless of what happens in the marketplace! Other than that, it is virtually identical to the VRM of the early-1980s. Resurrected and repackaged this way, six-month, fully open mortgages quickly became one of the most popular mortgage vehicles of the mid-1980s.

Whether you are going the short-term or long-term route,

there are a number of important questions to ask about a lender and its interest rates. How long will the lender guarantee the rate? Depending on the lender and the state of the market, it could be as short as 21 days or as long as 90 days, with 60-day commitments being the norm. But a 21-day guarantee period is little consolation to a purchaser whose closing is 90 days away.

What if rates rise or fall during that period? If the guarantee has any meaning whatsoever, the borrower should be protected from any increase in interest rates during the commitment period. But a fall in interest rates is a different story altogether. Some institutional lenders give their borrowers the benefit of a drop in interest rates between the date of the mortgage commitment, and the date the mortgage funds are advanced. Other lenders, especially private lenders, don't. Some lenders will allow only one rate reduction after the commitment is issued, while others permit an unlimited number. And still others will reduce the interest rate, provided the borrower pays an administrative fee. If that is the case, what is the fee?

These are important considerations, especially during a period of falling interest rates. Borrowers who can't take advantage of a decline in interest rates effectively are penalized for applying early for a loan. Neil and Jane applied for a mortgage 60 days before their June 20th closing, and were told the rate would be 12%. Al and Lorna applied for their mortgage 30 days before their June 20th closing, when rates had fallen to 11.5%. If Neil and Jane don't get the benefit of the drop in the rates, applying early for the loan cost them money. In this situation the early bird may get the worm, but the later bird got the lower interest rate! Of course the reverse is true during a period of rising interest rates.

If you can benefit from a drop in the rates, when will the final rate be set? This is an important consideration, especially when interest rates are on a roller-coaster ride. John and Dianne's mortgage commitment set a rate of 12%. During the 60-day guarantee period rates fell to 11.5%, but rose to 11.75% the week before closing. John and Dianne were told that if interest rates were *lower* than 12% the day before closing, they would benefit from the drop in rates. Therefore the rate charged to them was 11.75%. But John and Dianne did not benefit from *the lowest* interest rate during the 60-day period (11.5%). As they learned, "lower" does not mean "the lowest."

When Shopping for the Perfect Mortgage, Ask:

1) What is the interest rate for a particular mortgage term?
2) How long will the lender guarantee the interest rate?
3) Will you benefit from a drop in interest rates before closing? Is there any restriction on the number of rate reductions? Will there be any cost to obtain the lower rate?
4) If you get the benefit of a drop in rates, when will the "final" rate be set?

5
How is Your Interest Calculated?

A simple word could save you money

The cost of carrying a mortgage is high enough. Why face additional, unnecessary expenses that can be easily avoided? The key is to ensure the interest rate on a mortgage is calculated semi-annually (or its equivalent—half-yearly), not in advance. Incorrect information on how a mortgage is calculated, or a misplaced word, could cost thousands of dollars.

What does the expression "calculated semi-annually, not in advance" mean? First, there is absolutely no link between how often the interest is calculated and how often the mortgage is paid. Mortgages can be paid weekly, biweekly or semi-monthly, and still be calculated semi-annually, not in advance.

Let's start by examining the concept "not in advance." Compare a mortgage where Joe is the borrower, against the rent Moe pays as a tenant. When Moe pays his rent on February 1, he pays it "in advance" for the month to come—February. Who gets to invest the money during this month? The landlord, of course.

Joe, the homeowner, pays his mortgage "not in advance." The payment for the month of February is not made on February 1; that would be a payment in advance. Instead, Joe makes his mortgage payment for February on March 1—not in advance. This means Joe, the borrower, gets the use of the money during the month of February. When Joe paid his mortgage on February 1, that too was paid "not in advance" for the month that had gone by—January. "Not in advance," then, refers to when the payments are due. Since Canadian mortgages generally are payable "not in advance," ensure this is the case when shopping for the perfect mortgage.

What does "calculated semi-annually" mean (the expressions "calculated" and "compounded" being interchangeable)? *The more often interest is calculated during a year, the greater the yield to the*

22

lender and the more expensive the loan for the borrower. Loans calculated monthly produce a higher effective annual interest rate for a lender (and cost borrowers more) than loans calculated semi-annually. And loans calculated semi-annually produce a higher effective annual interest rate for a lender (and cost borrowers more) than loans calculated annually. The effective annual interest rate is the common measure for all loans—the rate of interest a lender earns at the end of a year. For example:

- 12% calculated *monthly* has an equivalent effective annual interest rate of 12.6825%;
- 12% calculated *semi-annually* has an equivalent effective annual interest rate of 12.36%;
- 12% calculated *annually* has an equivalent effective annual interest rate of 12%.

Remember: *the more often interest is calculated during a year, the greater the yield to the lender, and the more expensive the loan for the borrower.* Interest rates calculated monthly are best for the lender and worst for the borrower.

Loans where the frequency of payments and the interest calculation coincide (both monthly) generate the most interest for lenders. Car loans and personal loans fall into this category. To determine the rate of interest charged to borrowers when interest is calculated monthly and the blended payment is due monthly, simply divide the stated interest rate by 12. If the interest rate on Ron and Jennie's loan is 12% per annum calculated monthly, the amount charged to them each month is 12% divided by 12, or 1% per month. This 1% per month is the monthly interest factor for this loan, producing an effective annual interest rate of 12.6825% for the lender.

How do borrowers benefit from interest rates calculated semi-annually? Because an interest rate calculated every six months is cheaper than one calculated every month. Where the rate is 12% per annum calculated semi-annually, one-half of the rate (or 6%) is collected by the lender semi-annually (every six months). Since the payments will be made more frequently (monthly, weekly or biweekly) than the interest is calculated (semi-annually), an interest factor must be determined. The correct monthly interest factor is one which, when compounded six times, produces 6% after six months. For an interest rate of 12% calculated semi-annually, the monthly interest factor must be somewhat less than 1% per month, as that is the interest factor where the rate of 12% is calculated monthly. For a 12%

mortgage calculated semi-annually, the correct monthly interest factor is 0.9758794179%, a number that appears on the amortization schedule on page 135.

In the United States, mortgage interest is calculated monthly. In Canada, mortgage interest generally is calculated semi-annually. This means American mortgage amortization tables are inappropriate for most Canadian mortgages. More importantly, for the same stated rate of interest (say 12%), a mortgage calculated monthly (as in the U.S.) is more expensive than a mortgage calculated semi-annually (as in Canada)!

According to the Interest Act of Canada, when blended payments are made the stated interest rate must be calculated either semi-annually, not in advance, or annually, not in advance. Few lenders opt for the second choice as it generates a lower yield for the lender. But just because most lenders calculate their mortgages semi-annually does not mean lenders must do that, even to comply with the Interest Act of Canada.

Lenders can legally quote interest rates calculated quarterly, monthly, or even daily. Most second mortgages, loans with finance companies or credit unions, and *even some first mortgages* carry interest rates calculated monthly, not in advance. To comply with the Interest Act of Canada, Canadian lenders charging interest calculated monthly must state right in the mortgage the equivalent interest rate calculated semi-annually. In Ron and Jennie's case, the mortgage stated that the interest rate was 12% calculated monthly, not in advance, which was equivalent to 12.304% calculated semi-annually, not in advance.

What a difference a word makes. Because the loan was calculated "monthly" rather than "semi-annually," Ron and Jennie pay over 0.3% per year more in interest costs! Instead of a monthly payment of $1,031.90 as shown on page 135, Ron and Jennie will now be paying over $20 more per month, $1,053.22. Amortized over 25 years, the cost of carrying that mortgage jumps from $209,569.28 to $215,967.24. All because of one word!

To eliminate the confusion, a common yardstick is needed against which the true cost of borrowing can be compared. Otherwise, trying to analyze the same stated interest rate calculated in different ways means comparing apples with oranges. What's needed is the adoption of the Effective Annual Interest Rate (EAIR) for *all* types of loans (mortgage, car, business and personal). No matter how often the loan is paid or the interest rate calculated, the EAIR would show the true interest rate being borne by the borrower and earned by the lender *each year*. It would avoid the bewilderment of supposed 12% loans actually costing 12.36% (if calculated semi-annually) or 12.6825% (if calculated monthly). In the absence of the EAIR, calculating the real annual rate of interest on a loan is virtually impossible.

Since 1974, the interest rate quoted for all loans in the United Kingdom is the "annual percentage rate," the British name for the EAIR. Borrowers in the U.K. can immediately determine the real rate of interest being paid at the end of the year. Meanwhile, we here in Canada continue to muddle through a morass of different methods of calculating interest rates, with no end in sight. Certainly the time has come for what the Americans call "truth in lending," to ensure full and proper disclosure of the true cost of borrowing.

Don't be alarmed if the fine points of interest calculations escape you. Just remember one point—*an interest rate calculated semi-annually (say 12%) is cheaper than the same stated rate (12%) calculated monthly*. Therefore, be absolutely certain the interest rate is calculated semi-annually, not in advance. Anything else means the mortgage will be even more expensive than expected. Anything else may make you think twice about dealing with that lender.

Unless otherwise indicated, interest rates used in this book are calculated semi-annually, not in advance—the typical way residential mortgage rates are quoted in Canada.

When Shopping for the Perfect Mortgage, Ask:

1) How is the interest rate calculated (preferably *semi-annually* rather than monthly)?
2) Be sure payments are made "not in advance," at the end of the period rather than at the beginning.

6
Interest Adjustment Dates

A potential cash-flow killer

Whether refinancing an existing loan or arranging a new mortgage for a home purchase, one of the most important questions to ask when shopping for the perfect mortgage involves the "interest adjustment date" or IAD, the day the mortgage effectively begins to run. Where an IAD is used, the date the mortgage funds are advanced can create a "timing" problem for borrowers. Not understanding how IADs work could devastate a borrower's carefully planned cash flow.

As we saw in Chapter 5, Canadian mortgages are paid "not in advance," at the conclusion of the month. The first mortgage payment should be one month after the deal closes.

Although most institutional lenders want to receive their payments on the first day of each month, not all mortgages are booked at that time. Mortgage funds are advanced every business day. If the payment must be made on the first of the month, the first mortgage payment then will be more than one month after closing. To tie these two ideas together—payments collected the first of the month and funds advanced every day of the month—lenders use a concept called the "interest adjustment date." In its simplest form, a borrower pays interest for the balance of the month of closing somewhat earlier than usual.

As part of their purchase, Jack and Elaine booked a $100,000, 12% mortgage which closed September 20. Payments are due on the first day of each month. For the moment, ignore the balance of September. Because payments are due the first of each month, the first regular mortgage payment (covering a complete month) will be November 1—slightly more than one month after closing. That payment, made "not in advance," will cover the interest owing for the month of October, the first full month they owed the money.

In Jack and Elaine's mortgage the "interest adjustment date," the effective starting date for the mortgage, is October 1. The IAD is defined as the first of the month *after* the mortgage funds are advanced (September 20). The first regular mortgage payment is due one month after the IAD or November 1, covering the interest for the month of October.

Now let's look at the month of September. It is a "broken" month as any payment made will not cover a whole month. Because they had the use of the lender's money during that time, Jack and Elaine are still responsible to pay interest during the interval from September 20 (the day the funds were advanced) to the IAD of October 1. The question is: how does the lender collect it?

Much to the annoyance of borrowers, many institutional lenders deduct the interest from the date of closing to the IAD from the mortgage advance, scooping this interest right off the top. Not only that, they calculate the interest daily, making the charge even more expensive for the borrower. In Jack and Elaine's case, the 11 days' interest from September 20 to the IAD totalled $361.64 ($100,000 times 12% divided by 365 times 11 days). As the interest to the IAD is being deducted at source, Jack and Elaine won't receive this money from the lender. To close the purchase, they need an extra $361.64 of their own money.

While this $361.64 is a legitimate charge, the question is: when should it be paid? This is the timing problem associated with interest adjustment dates. Technically speaking, the money is only due on the IAD of October 1, to cover the interest from the date of the advance to the IAD. Why then do some lenders deduct interest to the IAD on closing from the mortgage advance, before it is due? Because it's easier and more convenient. It avoids having to bill borrowers for interest just days after the mortgage is registered. On closing, Jack and Elaine will have paid the interest to the end of September. The first mortgage payment, November 1, will cover the month of October.

But not all lenders employ IADs. Some institutional lenders and virtually all private lenders make a full mortgage advance on the date of closing. Their willingness to accept mortgage payments any day of the month helps borrowers with their cash flow for closing. The first payment is due exactly one month after the mortgage funds are advanced. Jonathan and Karen's purchase/mortgage also was completed September 20. But since their lender did not use an IAD, their first regular mortgage payment was October 20. The cash-flow crunch Jack and Elaine faced was eliminated, as Jonathan and Karen did not face a deduction of interest to the IAD.

Of those lenders that use IADs, some (but too few) still make a full mortgage advance the day of closing. Then they bill the borrower on the IAD for interest properly owing from the day the funds were advanced to the IAD. Once again borrowers benefit by not having funds deducted on closing. Marty and Brenda's lender followed this approach for their purchase/mortgage which also closed September 20. That day the lender advanced the full amount of the mortgage. On the IAD of October 1, it billed Marty and Brenda the interest between September 20 and the IAD in the amount of $361.64. By doing this, Marty and Brenda had a bit of time to organize this money before paying it to their lender.

So far only mortgages arranged to finance a purchase have been considered. The problem with lenders deducting interest to the interest adjustment date is aggravated on a refinancing, when *both* the old lender and the new lender must be dealt with.

Cheryl also refinanced her existing $100,000 mortgage on September 20. In her new mortgage the IAD was October 1, and her lender planned to deduct the interest to the IAD at source, right off the mortgage advance. The last regular payment to the old lender on the old mortgage was September 1, covering the month of August. The first regular mortgage payment on the new loan would be November 1, for the month of October.

What type of cash-flow problems did Cheryl face? First, the old lender was entitled to interest on its mortgage for the 19 days in September until the loan was paid off. With a rate of 12%, that would total $624.66 ($100,000 times 12% divided by 365 times 19 days). While this really should be calculated semi-annually following the mortgage, it is often calculated monthly when applied to a broken month. This money must be paid to the old lender when the loan is retired, on September 20.

In addition, on September 20 Cheryl's new lender will be charging her interest to the October 1 IAD in the amount of $361.64. Cheryl's dilemma is that the mortgage payment that normally would have been made October 1 to cover the month of September effectively is being made 11 days earlier, on September 20.

Whether the mortgage is being arranged for a purchase or a refinancing, closing even earlier in the month (say September 10th) would only compound the borrower's cash-flow problem. For anyone refinancing an existing loan, interest for the entire month of September that is otherwise due October 1 would be paid to both the old and new lenders 21 days earlier. Purchasers facing a lender that does not bill for interest to the IAD may find themselves paying interest to their new lender for the broken month of September almost a month ahead of schedule.

There is some limited consolation where an IAD is used and the accruing interest is deducted from the mortgage advance. Although borrowers like Jack and Elaine or Cheryl may face a cash-flow crisis for closing, no mortgage payment will have to be made until November 1. But that may mean little to those borrowers who find themselves short of funds for closing.

If the lender insists on deducting interest to the IAD from the mortgage advance, calculating the figure is relatively straightforward. Just as Jack and Elaine did, multiply the amount borrowed by the interest rate, divide that figure by 365 and multiply the result by the number of days from the day the funds are advanced to the IAD. The final figure is the amount of money the lender will be withholding at source.

The perfect mortgage would ignore the concept of interest adjustment dates, meaning a lender would collect its payments any day of the month starting one month after closing. But if the lender insists on receiving its money on a fixed date such as the first of the month, learn when interest to the IAD must be paid—on closing or the actual IAD. The answer to this question could sway you into choosing one lender over another, if all other factors are identical.

When Shopping for the Perfect Mortgage, Ask:

1) Does the lender provide a full mortgage advance on closing, or does it use an interest adjustment date?
2) If the lender uses an IAD, does it deduct the interest to the IAD on closing from the mortgage advance? Or does it bill the borrower on the IAD for interest to the IAD?

7
The Importance of Prepayment Privileges

Don't book a mortgage without them

One of the most important features to include when booking the perfect mortgage is prepayment privileges. The right decision will provide you with the maximum in flexibility, whether you take a long-term or short-term mortgage, whether interest rates go up, stay stable or fall, and whether you sell your home during the mortgage term or renew the mortgage on maturity. The wrong choice inevitably will cost money, usually thousands of dollars.

Even though we don't know what the future holds in store, we can build the right safeguards and protections into our mortgages to cover what is reasonably possible. This way the appropriate options are already in place, allowing for a change of direction at nominal, or no, cost. The downside risk of doing anything else is just too great. Therefore, it is absolutely essential for borrowers to include in their mortgages the best prepayment features available in the marketplace.

There are four different ways to prepay a mortgage:
- Reducing the amortization;
- Increasing the regular payment;
- Paying the mortgage more often than monthly;
- Paying a lump sum towards the outstanding principal.

This chapter will examine the importance of including prepayment privileges in your mortgage. Following chapters will contain detailed examinations of each of these four ways to pay off your principal sooner—and save money.

A term often associated with prepayment privileges is "open." But there is considerable confusion about what is an "open" mortgage. In its simplest form, a mortgage is a contract. A certain sum of money must be repaid punctually—no more and no less. By their very nature mortgages are "closed," not allowing any additional money to be paid (other than the regular payment) before the mortgage matures.

Any right to pay additional money towards the mortgage before it otherwise becomes due (the so-called prepayment privilege) must be clearly spelled out in the mortgage. Sometimes a penalty is levied when the open clause is invoked, sometimes not. Inevitably the right of borrowers to make a lump-sum prepayment during the term of a mortgage was dubbed the "open" privilege.

Prepayments not only reduce the amortization for the mortgage, but also its overall interest cost. Consider the $100,000 mortgage Marshall and Shelley arranged carrying a 12% interest rate and amortized over 25 years, appearing on page 135. If Marshall and Shelley prepaid $2,000 together with payment 12, the total amortization for the loan will fall from 25 years to 22.682 years. Meanwhile, the total interest cost of the loan (in after-tax dollars) is shaved from $209,569.28 to $182,872.08.

How does this work? The entire lump-sum prepayment made with payment 12 is applied to directly reduce the amount of the outstanding principal. As a rent charge, interest is only paid on the amount of money owing. If $2,000 less is owing, then less interest is owing for payment 13 than would otherwise be the case. But as the payment is blended, remaining constant despite the prepayment, a smaller component of the payment will be interest than would otherwise be the case, while a larger part of the payment will be principal. In other words, the $2,000 prepayment not only reduces the outstanding principal, but it also means that principal will be reduced faster than normal, in the future. Coupled with the prepayment itself, this accelerated reduction in principal results in a significant savings for borrowers.

Over the years financial institutions have softened the harshness of the closed mortgage by gratuitously including some type of prepayment clause in their mortgages. Lenders now heavily market these prepayment features as a means of attracting new business. This heightened competition means better prepayment features are available today for consumers than a decade ago.

But different mortgages have different degrees of "openness." "Open" mortgages allow *some* of the principal to be prepaid before it would otherwise be payable to the lender. "Fully open" permits *all* of the principal to be prepaid before the mortgage comes due. Some mortgages are more open than others.

Just because a mortgage is "open" does not necessarily mean it is "fully open," allowing the entire amount to be prepaid at any time before the mortgage matures. It could be just "partially open," meaning the balance is "closed." The question is: how "open" is "open"?

To better understand the difference between a fully open mortgage and one just partially open (with the balance being closed), compare a mortgage with a door. At one extreme it is fully open (and no part of it is closed), allowing borrowers to pay back as much or as little as they want, whenever they like. At the other extreme it is fully closed, not open at all, permitting no additional funds to be paid to the lender.

For most of its swing the door (and also the mortgage) is partially open—and also partially closed. If the door is 10% open, it is 90% closed. And if the door is 25% open, 75% of it is closed. Just because it's open does not necessarily mean it is fully open. In other words, to whatever extent the mortgage is not open, it is closed. The vast majority of residential Canadian mortgages are "partially open," where the door is partway open but also partially closed. And that means there is no automatic right to prepay the rest of the mortgage.

Besides the open/closed dilemma, borrowers are also concerned about penalties for prepaying a mortgage. Contrary to generally accepted public thinking, there is no automatic right to fully pay off any mortgage by paying the lender a penalty of three months' interest, except in very limited circumstances examined in the next chapter. The problems with prepayment penalties are intertwined with this open/closed dilemma.

Fully open mortgages clearly state right in the mortgage what the penalty will be (if any) if borrowers exercise the prepayment privilege. That is the very essence of a fully open mortgage— knowing at the outset what it will cost to break the contract, in whole or in part. Any penalty to be charged is predetermined when the mortgage is arranged.

By contrast, borrowers with *partially open* mortgages (where the balance of the mortgage is closed) find themselves in a very weak bargaining position with very few rights. To the extent the mortgage is open (often 10% or 15% annually), the cost of prepaying the mortgage is spelled out. But to the extent the mortgage is closed (the remaining 85% to 90%), the mortgage is silent about what the prepayment penalty will be. Ten percent or 15% may be good, but it certainly isn't 100%. What about the rest of the mortgage? That remaining 85% or 90% remains closed, with no advance prepayments allowed.

Too many people confuse a mortgage that allows 10% or 15% of the principal to be prepaid each year with a "fully open" mortgage. Too often they discover the difference after signing an offer to sell their house but before the actual closing. Imagine the shock of learning this open privilege only allows part but not all the total outstanding mortgage to be paid off early. Too often borrowers in these circumstances are then told by their lender: "Sit down—let's talk about the penalty." Those are words no borrower wants to hear!

Many times the real need to fully prepay a mortgage only arises when a property has been sold and the purchaser does not want to take over the mortgage. But prepayment clauses are not the exclusive concern of sellers. With mortgage interest costs generally being nondeductible from other income (and paid in "after-tax" dollars), all borrowers should pay off their principal as soon as possible to reduce the high interest costs. Small amounts prepaid towards a mortgage, especially in the early years, result in large interest savings over time. But the only way to do this, of course, is to have a mortgage with the best prepayment privileges possible.

What is the biggest problem having a closed or just a partially open mortgage? It's the uncertainty the borrower faces about what the lender will do with the closed portion of the mortgage. Unless the mortgage is 100% open, borrowers refinancing or, more important, selling their homes during the term of the mortgage will be unsure:

a) whether the entire mortgage can even be prepaid! Yes, lenders can veto an early retirement of the closed portion of the loan! and

b) the cost of prepaying the mortgage, if the lender decides to allow it. The lender alone determines how hefty the penalty will be, meaning it can exact whatever arbitrary sum it wants. There are no safeguards to protect borrowers against exorbitant penalties.

Obviously, insufficient information about prepayment privileges when booking a mortgage could lead to an unpleasant surprise in the future when trying to pay it off.

This uncertainty makes it very difficult to properly budget when selling a property, as so much depends on how the lender exercises its arbitrary powers. Since the questions weren't properly answered when the mortgage was booked, they now have to be dealt with at the worst possible moment for a borrower—when the actual prepayment is about to take place.

To eliminate these problems, when shopping for the perfect mortgage borrowers should look for (and book) a mortgage with the most liberal prepayment privileges. The chapters that follow will describe the significant variations in lump-sum prepayment privileges, as well as other options that will reduce the high cost of mortgage financing. Remember, these features apply equally whether a mortgage is being arranged to finance a purchase, or to refinance an existing loan. The time to inquire, examine and analyze is now, before any mortgage papers are signed. When it comes to prepayment privileges, understand fully what you are committing to before making that commitment.

When Shopping for the Perfect Mortgage:

Be sure you understand the distinction between a fully open and a partially open mortgage. Not all "open" clauses are the same. Remember, a mortgage is closed, meaning the lender does not even have to accept a prepayment of the loan, unless open privileges appear right in the mortgage document.

8
Open vs. Closed Mortgages

How open is your mortgage?

As we saw in the last chapter, different mortgages are open to different degrees. When shopping for the perfect mortgage, borrowers must learn if the mortgage is open, to what extent it is open, and what the prepayment penalties will be (if any). This is important, since the prepayment privileges offered by the major institutional lenders today are literally all over the map.

Lump-sum prepayment privileges fit neatly into five categories. Variations between and within each category help distinguish different lenders' packages. Be absolutely certain the prepayment privileges are in writing, and appear right in the mortgage. Being told the lender's "policy" includes one of these prepayment features is not good enough. Policy can change overnight. Starting with what's best for borrowers, mortgages can be any one of the following.

1) Fully open, with no penalty or notice.
2) Open, with a predetermined penalty or notice.
3) Limited (partially) open, with no penalty or notice on that open portion.
4) Limited (partially) open, with a predetermined penalty or notice on that open portion.
5) Fully closed.

1) Fully Open, with No Penalty or Notice
This is the best type of open privilege borrowers can arrange. While it's the least readily available, fully open mortgages are far from a rarity today. Many major financial institutions offer fully open mortgages with terms of six months or one year. But they also carry a higher interest rate than a "closed" mortgage with the same term (an additional 0.5% or more).

With this type of mortgage, the entire principal or any part of it can be prepaid to the lender at any time, without having to pay any penalty or bonus interest to the lender. No prior notice has to be given, either.

2) Open, with a Predetermined Penalty or Notice
Just as in category 1, all or part of the principal can be prepaid at any time. But here, the lender wants to be compensated for taking back the money early. What the borrower must pay is a predetermined penalty clearly spelled out right in the mortgage, or give a set amount of written notice. Nothing has to be negotiated when the prepayment is made; the amount of the lender's compensation (or notice) was fixed when the mortgage was booked. While this mortgage is 100% open, meaning the total amount can be prepaid at any time, it is not "fully open" in the accepted sense of the word—without any penalty being levied by the lender. Often the preset penalty included in the mortgage is three months' bonus, although it could be more, or less, or based on some type of formula.

Recently this category of prepayment privileges has increased in popularity. Some institutional lenders put the privilege in category 3 for part of the mortgage term (perhaps the first four years of a five-year mortgage) and then shift it to category 2 for the last year. Others may have a category 3 privilege for part of the borrowed money, and category 2 for the rest.

A serious move is now under way to put all residential mortgages in category 2—100% open with a predetermined penalty that can be eliminated in many cases. Mortgages with this type of prepayment penalty are not just theoretical; they are presently available from some lenders. The name for this exciting, new idea in open mortgages: the interest rate differential, a topic examined in Chapter 12.

As the prepayment penalty is prearranged before the mortgage is booked, borrowers never face a lender's "whim and discretion" when prepaying the mortgage. If unable to arrange a loan in category 1, borrowers seeking the perfect mortgage should ensure their prepayment privilege falls here.

3) Limited (Partially) Open, with No Penalty or Notice on That Open Portion
This is far and away the most common category for residential mortgages in Canada today. And it is one of the "10s" for a "10 plus 10" (or one of the 15s for a "15 plus 15") mortgage

readily available in the marketplace. The first number deals with the lump-sum prepayment privilege, while the other has to do with increasing the mortgage payment, as discussed in Chapter 10.

Here the mortgage is partially open, but not fully open. In fact, more of the mortgage is closed than open. By contractual agreement the mortgage permits a limited, fixed percentage to be returned to the lender each year (up to 10% or 15%, depending on the lender), in addition to the regular payment without any penalty being paid or notice being given. *However, this specified contractual open privilege only applies to a specified portion of the mortgage—10% or 15% annually.* Silence about the rest of the mortgage means the other 85% or 90% is closed! No wonder some people call this a "closed" mortgage.

Borrowers anxious to prepay the open portion of a category 3 mortgage can do so without incurring any penalty. Unfortunately that is not the case for the balance of the mortgage, the closed portion. The prearranged waiver of penalty only applies to a maximum of 10% or 15% of the loan each year.

Since the balance of the mortgage is closed, it can only be prepaid if the lender allows—and then on the lender's terms! Since there is no obligation on the lender's part to accept an early repayment, the penalty exacted can be as arbitrary and unreasonable as the lender wants! Whether the closed portion of the mortgage can be prepaid and if so, at what cost, depends on the "whim and discretion" of the lender. Borrowers find it impossible to negotiate from strength, since the penalty for prepaying the closed part of the mortgage must be negotiated at the last minute, when the prepayment takes place. All borrowers can do is grin and bear it, and pay the demanded charge.

When arranging a mortgage, be sure to distinguish between the contractual right to prepay the *open* portion of a category 3 mortgage, and the need to negotiate a penalty when prepaying the *closed* portion of a category 3 mortgage. Too many people believe their mortgages are "fully" open, only to learn they are just "limited open," and the rest of the mortgage closed. While those borrowers can utilize the 10% open privilege, what do they do about the remaining closed 90%, the part not spelled out in the loan?

4) Limited (Partially) Open, with a Predetermined Penalty or Notice on That Open Portion

Category 4 is a hybrid of categories 2 and 3. Like a mortgage in category 3, it is partially open—often up to 10% or 15% annually. Like category 2 and unlike category 3, a predetermined interest penalty (usually three months' interest) must be paid to the lender, or a fixed amount of written notice must be given by the borrower, to invoke that prepayment privilege. *However, that specified contractual penalty only applies to a limited portion of the mortgage—a maximum of 10% or 15% each year.* Once again, as the mortgage is silent about prepayment privileges for the remaining 85% or 90% of the mortgage, that portion of the mortgage is closed, and does not allow an automatic early prepayment of the loan! Because of this, some people also dub it a "closed" mortgage.

Since most of the mortgage is closed, just as in category 3 the lender can charge any penalty it wants when that part of the mortgage is prepaid, or even refuse to permit the prepayment! Once again, the penalty must be negotiated when the prepayment of the closed portion takes place, rather than being preset when the loan was arranged. This is definitely not the best of situations for a borrower.

5) Fully Closed

This is the worst scenario for a borrower—no right at all to prepay the mortgage! All mortgages fall into this category unless prepayment privileges appear right in the mortgage. As the entire category 5 loan is closed during the term of the mortgage, no part of the outstanding principal can be paid before maturity, and there is no obligation by the lender to accept the money! Only the regular payments can be made to the lender—nothing more. If the lender agrees to accept the outstanding money before it falls due, the lender has the absolute discretion to decide what penalty the borrower will pay for breaking the contract. The borrower has little room in which to manoeuvre; nothing was predetermined before the loan was arranged.

Besides this, one other important prepayment privilege should be kept in mind. *No matter what the lenders say, all mortgages are fully open on their maturity.* This means that all or part of the outstanding principal can be paid when the mortgage comes due, without having to pay any prepayment penalty whatsoever.

QUESTIONS AND ANSWERS ON PREPAYING YOUR MORTGAGE

Many factors within each category determine how much can be prepaid, and when. Because no two mortgage lenders offer the exact same package of prepayment features, a myriad of variations exists in today's marketplace. While the differences may appear small, the consequences for borrowers could be substantial.

What are these distinguishing features that could affect the selection of both a mortgage and a mortgage lender?

Is there a maximum that can be prepaid?
The "degree of openness" in categories 3 and 4 varies from lender to lender. (Categories 1 and 2, of course, are 100% open, while category 5 is not open at all.) Most allow borrowers, at their option, to prepay a maximum annual amount of up to 10% or 15%, but higher and lower percentages do exist.

Most lenders base the percentage on the original amount borrowed (which benefits borrowers) rather than the amount currently outstanding, which is a constantly declining figure. With a 10% prepayment privilege in their $100,000 mortgage, George and Pauline could prepay the same maximum ($10,000) each year regardless of the amount owed at the time of the prepayment. On the other hand, because Mark and Angela could only prepay 10% of what they *owed* at any given time, they could only prepay $7,500 that year when their outstanding balance had dropped to $75,000.

Is there a minimum that must be prepaid?
Because lenders want to avoid processing small prepayments, they often fix a minimum amount that must be prepaid in order to utilize the prepayment privilege. This could apply to borrowers in categories 1 and 2, or 3 and 4 (up to the permitted maximum). Depending on the lender, it could be $100, $500 or even $1,000. Others require that the prepayment be made in multiples of $100, for ease in administration.

Is the prepayment privilege cumulative or noncumulative?
Once again this is a concern for borrowers with mortgages in categories 3 and 4 only. If a borrower does not use his or her entire prepayment privilege one year, can he or she apply the unused portion the following year? In most cases the answer is no, the privilege is noncumulative, and the unused portion is

lost forever. If Arnold and Hyla only prepay $6,500 of their $9,000 permitted maximum in one year, they cannot add the remaining $2,500 on to next year's limit in order to prepay $11,500.

Must a prepayment be made in accordance with the amortization schedule for the mortgage?
Consider this when a mortgage falls into categories 1, 2, 3 and 4, subject to the allowable limit in the last two categories. Some lenders, especially noninstitutional ones, want to avoid ordering a new computer schedule every time a prepayment is made. By requiring that any prepayment follow the amortization schedule, the old schedule remains valid despite the prepayment.

For a prepayment to be valid according to the amortization schedule, the additional funds must be paid on the same day as the regular payment. Most clauses requiring prepayments according to the amortization schedule say just that.

How do borrowers like Michael and Judy make a prepayment according to the amortization schedule? Consider the schedule appearing on page 135. After making payment 11 on December 1, 1989, Michael and Judy still owe $99,352.80. To prepay using the schedule, they add up the appropriate number of items under the principal column, starting with line 12. If they wanted to prepay roughly $1,000, Michael and Judy would add up the *principal* components only of lines 12 through 26 (ignoring the interest column and all other columns), and arrive at a figure of $1,001.69. This would be the amount prepaid on December 1, 1989. Line 27 would now represent the breakdown of principal and interest for the payment due on January 1, 1990, the new 12th payment. While the dates of the following payments must be changed, the schedule itself would still be valid.

How often can the mortgage be prepaid?
Usually borrowers are allowed to prepay their mortgages just once a year. Others allow two prepayments a year, while still others permit the mortgage to be prepaid an unlimited number of times, provided the maximum percentage is not exceeded. This question is of concern to anyone with a mortgage in categories 3 and 4 only, although it would restrict the 100% open privilege for mortgages in categories 1 and 2.

When can the mortgage be prepaid?
Once again borrowers with mortgages in the first four categories
must address this issue. When dealing with the timing of prepayments, several different questions must be answered. One
of those: does the mortgage require that any prepayments be
made only on the same day as a regular payment? In more and
more cases the answer is yes.

In fact, an increasing number of category 1 and 2 loans (100%
open) are also facing this contractual restriction. Originally these
mortgages could be prepaid at any time whatsoever. While lenders are entitled to interest to the actual date of payment, properly
accounting between principal and interest for a mid-month prepayment is difficult. Hence the shift to prepayments on a regular
payment date *only*, even for fully open loans. While borrowers
should try to avoid clauses that limit prepayments to one day a
month, they should consider *voluntarily* prepaying their mortgages on a payment date.

There is one major exception to this rule of thumb. When
a house is being sold and the mortgage is being fully paid off,
the earlier the prepayment the better. Prepayments only on
payment dates will cost borrowers money. In Harry and
Linda's mortgage, a prepayment could only be made on a payment date, the first day of each month. When they sold their
home on June 15th, Harry and Linda had to pay interest up
to July 1—an additional penalty, effectively, of half a month's
interest.

*If prepayments are permitted once a year, who decides the date—the
lender or the borrower?*
This very important question is often overlooked. Assuming that
only one prepayment is allowed each year, can the prepayment
only take place on a date fixed by the lender or can the mortgage
be prepaid on any payment date selected by the borrower? The
distinction is significant.

Years ago, most lenders allowed one prepayment *on one specific
day each year*, the anniversary of the interest adjustment date of
the mortgage. Gord and Connie booked a three-year mortgage
on August 27, 1989, with an IAD of September 1, 1989. This
restriction meant Gord and Connie could prepay their mortgage
on just two days, September 1, 1990 and September 1, 1991.
On September 1, 1992, of course, the mortgage matured and

the loan was fully open. The mortgage prevented Gord and Connie from prepaying the mortgage on any other days during the mortgage term. If Gord and Connie got a Christmas bonus from work in 1989, they could not prepay it towards the mortgage until September 1, 1990, more than eight months later. Some lenders still take this approach today.

Many other lenders have liberalized this rule, and as a result borrowers are not limited to prepaying their mortgages on just one specific date each year. While they can still prepay their mortgage just once each mortgage year, *borrowers can exercise the privilege on any one of the 12 regular payment dates during the course of the mortgage year*. (In Gord and Connie's case the mortgage year would run from September 1 to August 31, beginning with the interest adjustment date.)

While Gord and Connie still can prepay their mortgage only once each mortgage year, the number of opportunities to do that has increased 12 times. During their three-year term Gord and Connie could prepay their mortgage three times, once from September 1, 1989 to August 31, 1990; once from September 1, 1990 to August 31, 1991; and once from September 1, 1991 to August 31, 1992. All payments, of course, would have to be on a regular payment date, the first of the month. With this clause, Gord and Connie could prepay their 1989 Christmas bonus on January 1, 1990, and have it start saving additional interest from that day forward.

Some lenders have gone even further by substituting a *calendar* year for a *mortgage* year. This gives borrowers one additional opportunity to prepay their mortgage, even when restricted to a payment date. If Gord and Connie could prepay their mortgage once each calendar year, they would have *four* opportunities during their three-year term—once in 1989, once in 1990, once in 1991, and once in 1992 before maturity—with all prepayments to be on a regular payment date, the first of the month. On maturity the mortgage could also be prepaid in full.

One other minor qualification usually applies—that the mortgage not be in default at the time the prepayment is made. Be careful of clauses that deny the right to prepay if the borrower has *ever* been in default. *One late payment and the prepayment privilege in the mortgage is lost forever.*

When does the prepayment privilege begin?
A category 1 to 4 concern. Not all prepayment privileges begin when the funds are advanced. In some mortgages a specified period of time must pass, such as one or two years following the interest adjustment date, before the prepayment privilege begins. During that period of time, the mortgage effectively is in category 5!

OTHER POINTS TO KEEP IN MIND
Besides these questions dealing with the specifics of prepayment clauses, keep several other points in mind.

I What is the usual penalty when a borrower wishes to prepay the "open" portion of a "closed" mortgage?
Categories 3 and 4 are being considered here, and in particular the limited prepayment privilege lenders offer gratuitously to borrowers. If no penalty is charged on the amount covered by the privilege (up to 10% or 15% annually of the amount borrowed), as is usually the case, the loan falls into category 3. If a penalty is levied on the "limited open" portion of the loan, it's a category 4 loan. Where this applies, three months' bonus interest on the amount prepaid is the normal charge, although some private lenders do charge lower penalties for short-term loans. Remember, whether or not a penalty is charged is a contractual term appearing right in the mortgage. It is not a matter for negotiation, *and it only applies to the "open" part of the "closed" mortgage.* As the rest of the mortgage is closed, it cannot be prepaid.

How is "three months' bonus interest" calculated? It does not mean the penalty is three times the mortgage payment, which includes interest and principal. Instead, what must be multiplied by three is the interest component of the upcoming mortgage payment. Marvin and Debbie's mortgage, which appears on page 135, allows them to prepay up to 10% annually on any payment date upon paying three months' bonus interest. After 30 months, when the amount outstanding on the mortgage was $98,058.41, they decided to prepay $5,000. As that prepayment represented 5.099% of the total amount outstanding, the penalty paid should be 5.099% of the total penalty payable if the mortgage was retired in full.

Although the regular monthly payment is $1,031.90, the penalty should *not* be $1,031.90 times three times 5.099%, or $185.43. Instead, the penalty was based on the upcoming interest component only. To pay off the entire mortgage, the penalty would be $956.93 (the interest component for payment 31) times three, or $2,870.79. To pay off 5.099% of the mortgage, the penalty would be $2,870.79 times 5.099% or $146.38.

II What is the usual penalty when a borrower wishes to prepay the "closed" portion of a "closed" mortgage?
This is the dilemma facing borrowers with loans in categories 3, 4 and 5. Our concern here is not the penalty to be paid on the "limited open" portion (10% or 15% annually) of a mortgage in categories 3 and 4, as that is specifically dealt with right in the mortgage. Instead we are concerned about the closed portion of these loans—the remaining 85% to 90% of those mortgages, and the entire amount of a category 5 mortgage. These are not specifically covered by any prepayment clause in the mortgage.

Although a penalty of three months' interest is what lenders normally charge to pay off the closed portion of a closed mortgage, they are not limited by contract or by law to just that amount. Lenders have been permitted to exact penalties of six months' interest and even more when the closed portion of a closed mortgage is prepaid. Courts have said that lenders can charge any arbitrary penalty they want. Even all the interest up to the maturity date of the loan could be demanded (a windfall profit if there ever was one!), assuming the lender allows the prepayment in the first place. After all, it's the borrower who wants to break the mortgage, and the mortgage is silent on what penalty the lender can charge!

III Is there any statutory right to prepay a mortgage?
The only statutory right Canadian borrowers have to prepay their mortgages appears in Section 10 of the Interest Act (Canada) and comparable provincial legislation. These sections ensure that borrowers can pay off their mortgages at the end of each five-year period. Qualifying mortgages can only be retired in full (and not in part), and then only on payment of a three months' interest penalty. These sections impose a three-hurdle test that must be met before the statutory right to prepay applies:

1) Who booked the mortgage, an individual or a corporation? If the original borrower was an individual, the first hurdle is satisfied. If it was a corporation, no statutory right to prepay exists even if the current owner of the property is an individual who assumed the mortgage from a corporation, such as a builder.

2) Is the period of time from the signing of the original mortgage to its maturity more than five years? This is the key question to answer when trying to rely on the statutory right to prepay. The five-year clock starts to run the day the mortgage was signed. With very few mortgages today being written for terms longer than five years, how can some borrowers take advantage of this section? When interest adjustment dates are used, the mortgage could have been signed anywhere from one to 30 days before the IAD. This means a five-year mortgage could have an original term of *five years plus several additional days*, the extra time being the period from the signing of the mortgage to the interest adjustment date. Remember, too, that the time from signing to maturity—the original term—must be *more* than five years. If it is less than five years or exactly five years, no statutory right to prepay exists.

What about renewals? In a 1986 decision, the Supreme Court of Canada said renewals could be added to the original term of the mortgage to satisfy the "more than five years" requirement. At five years plus one day of original term and renewals, the borrower can retire the mortgage by paying the statutory penalty, even though the renewed mortgage has not yet matured.

3) Have at least five years passed since the mortgage was signed? On the surface, this would appear to be a relatively easy question. At least five years must have passed before the section becomes operative. In the typical situation, the statutory prepayment privilege is being invoked during the renewal term.

However, very few mortgages today qualify for the statutory right to prepay, even when renewed, because of lenders' legal gymnastics. Many lenders now insert clauses into mortgage renewals which, unknown to the borrower, re-date the mortgage at that time. These clauses deem the date the renewal was signed to be the "original" date of the mortgage. Effectively this means the third hurdle cannot be overcome, since five years have not passed since the mortgage was signed.

David and Jan took out a three-year mortgage on June 1, 1984, and renewed it for another three years in 1987. By June 1989, when more than five years had passed since the mortgage was booked, David and Jan thought they could prepay the mortgage by paying three months' interest penalty. But they couldn't, because the renewal agreement stated that the maturity date of their old loan (June 1, 1987) became the "original" date of the mortgage. Since only two years and not five had passed since that time, David and Jan had no statutory right to prepay. That same 1986 Supreme Court of Canada decision upheld lenders' actions changing the "original" date of the mortgage this way.

When shopping for the perfect mortgage, learn where a potential prepayment privilege falls. Categories 1 and 2 are the best for borrowers. To book a category 3, 4 or 5 mortgage and have no predetermined prepayment penalty for the entire mortgage means considerable uncertainty in the future as to whether it can be prepaid and if so, at what cost. No matter what they are called, they are little more than sugar-coated closed mortgages.

When Shopping for the Perfect Mortgage, Ask:

1) What are the lenders' prepayment privileges? How "open" is that mortgage?
2) Into which category does the mortgage fall:
    i) fully open, with no penalty or notice
    ii) open, with a predetermined penalty or notice
    iii) limited (partially) open, with no penalty or notice on that open portion
    iv) limited (partially) open, with a predetermined penalty or notice on that open portion
    v) fully closed
3) What other restrictions apply to the prepayment privilege:
    i) Is there a maximum that can be prepaid?
    ii) Is there a minimum that must be prepaid?

iii) Is the prepayment privilege cumulative or non-cumulative?

iv) Must a prepayment be made in accordance with the amortization schedule for the mortgage?

v) How often can the mortgage be prepaid?

vi) When can the mortgage be prepaid?

vii) If prepayments are limited to one payment date a year, who decides the date—the lender or the borrower? Is it based on a mortgage year or a calendar year?

viii) When does the prepayment privilege begin?

4) Is there any statutory right to prepay the mortgage?

9
Reducing the Amortization

Shorter amortizations save borrowers money

As we saw in Chapter 3, the amortization for a mortgage is the period of time it would take for the loan to be fully retired, assuming there were no prepayments (early payments) and no late payments. With mortgages, it's the length of time the debt is outstanding (the amortization period) rather than the interest rate that makes the loan expensive. If the loan can be paid off faster, it's going to save borrowers money.

Traditionally the amortization for Canadian mortgages is 25 years while it's 30 years in the United States. For generations Canadians have blindly accepted the 25-year amortization as if it were set in concrete. Rarely have they questioned if another alternative might be more advantageous. There is—a shorter amortization. It's an easy and simple way to prepay a mortgage and reduce its total interest cost. When it comes to amortizations, the less the better.

Shorter amortizations mean larger monthly (or weekly, bi-weekly or semi-monthly) mortgage payments, but lower overall interest costs. That statement is so important, it bears repeating. *Shorter amortizations mean larger mortgage payments, but lower overall interest costs.*

Howard and Doris arranged the $100,000, 12% mortgage that appears on page 135. As they amortized the loan over 25 years, the monthly payment was $1,031.90. Over the 25-year amortized life of this mortgage, they would pay $209,569.28 in interest, plus the $100,000 in principal they originally borrowed.

Aron and Frieda also booked a $100,000 mortgage at 12% per annum. But instead of accepting a 25-year amortization, they reduced it to 20 years. The new monthly payment was $1,080.97, or $49.07 more per month.

What was the impact of reducing the amortization from 25 to 20 years on the total interest cost of the loan? Tremendous.

Over the amortized life of this mortgage Aron and Frieda would pay $159,433.78 in interest, a savings of $50,135.50 or 23.9% of the interest cost Howard and Doris will incur.

All this saving is achieved by paying about $1.60 more towards the mortgage each day! This is not an enormous sum; it's half the cost of a pack of cigarettes a day, or roughly the price of a coffee and muffin. Because this interest was nondeductible, by being in the $33^1/_3\%$ tax bracket Aron and Frieda would also save over $25,000 in income tax on the $75,000 they would have had to earn just to pay that $50,000 interest. And by reducing the amortization from 25 years to 20 years, how many fewer years worth of mortgage payments do they face? Five years.

Never, never, never increase the amortization for a mortgage beyond 25 years. The savings in monthly payments are nominal compared to the additional costs incurred. If Howard and Doris booked a 30-year amortization, the monthly payment would fall from $1,031.90 to $1,006.39. But it would now take them another five years to pay off the mortgage, and the interest cost for the mortgage would inflate to $262,299.46. Considerable pain for little gain.

Despite the higher payments, shorter amortizations clearly are an important way for borrowers to pay off their principal sooner. Saving money this way doesn't require that you be a mathematical whiz. All you have to do is ask the lender for a 20-year amortization instead of the conventional 25-year option.

The key word here is "ask." Unless you specifically request a reduced amortization, the mortgage will automatically be booked at the 25-year level. Rare is the lender that will voluntarily offer or even suggest a 20-year amortization. Some lenders will reduce the amortization on request, but only in multiples of five. This means that 20-year and 15-year amortizations are fine, but not 18 or 23 years. And a few will still resist any change from the 25-year norm, arguing your request is unusual. Nonsense! Remember, to accelerate the retirement of your mortgage by shortening the amortization, the first move clearly is up to you.

Reducing the amortization doesn't apply only to the home buyer arranging a new mortgage to finance a purchase. Homeowners renewing or refinancing an existing mortgage benefit equally from paring down the amortization. In other words, shorter amortizations benefit everyone.

Obviously not all borrowers will be able to handle the higher payment that results from a mortgage with a reduced amortization. Paying more towards your mortgage when you don't have the financial resources could lead to financial suicide. But some people who can't do so today might be able to do it tomorrow, perhaps on a mortgage renewal.

Whenever possible consider reducing the amortization for your mortgage. It's a straightforward but effective way of reducing the high interest cost for a mortgage.

When Shopping for the Perfect Mortgage, Ask:

1) Can the amortization for the mortgage be reduced below 25 years?
2) If so, must it be a "round" number, in multiples of five, or can it be any amortization the borrower chooses?

10
Increasing Your Payment

Putting extra money to good use

So far we've looked at two ways to prepay a mortgage—lump-sum prepayments and shorter amortizations. The third way, a relatively recent development, allows borrowers to increase the mortgage payment over the term of the loan. Once again borrowers can save a considerable amount of money by prepaying small amounts towards their mortgage this way in the early years.

For decades lenders viewed mortgages as fixed rate, fixed payment contracts, allowing no change in the payment over the term of the mortgage. Understandably many borrowers like Darryl and Michelle questioned the lenders' stubbornness. The first mortgage payment, the hardest for most people to make, was the same as the last payment, some five years down the road. Over those five years Darryl and Michelle should receive a raise in salary. The extra money would cover increases in the cost of living, such as clothing, food and transportation. But the additional earnings could not be applied towards their mortgage payment; it was set for the entire mortgage term.

That is not the case today. Some lenders heavily market their "10 plus 10" or "15 plus 15" prepayment package. The first 10 (or 15) represents the lump-sum privilege discussed in Chapter 8. The second describes the right given to Darryl and Michelle to permanently increase or "boost" their regular mortgage payment by *up to* 10% (or by *up to* 15%) annually. Whether the payment is increased is strictly voluntary; it's an option only the borrower can exercise. Whether Darryl and Michelle take full advantage of the 10% or 15% option also rests with them. But what borrowers must remember is that not all lenders offer this "step-up" in payment feature. Some do, some don't; it all depends on the lender. Unless this right exists in the mortgage, the regular mortgage payment cannot be increased over time, and the payment for the first month will be identical to the last.

How does increasing the payment benefit Darryl and Michelle? Originally they booked the $100,000 mortgage appearing on page 135, which had a monthly payment of $1,031.90. They paid that amount each month for the first year, from February 1, 1989 to January 1, 1990. Each anniversary date after that Darryl and Michelle increased the previous year's payment by 5%. This meant that for the second year of the mortgage, starting with payment 13 (from February 1, 1990, to January 1, 1991), the new monthly payment was $1,083.50. During the third year of the mortgage, starting with payment 25 (from February 1, 1991, to January 1, 1992), the new monthly payment was $1,137.68. And so forth.

What was the impact on their mortgage? Enormous, since the entire increase in the monthly payment was applied to reduce the outstanding principal, which in turn decreased its amortization. Instead of paying off the loan in 25 years, by increasing the previous years' payment by 5% on each anniversary of the interest adjustment date, Darryl and Michelle retired their loan in just 12 years three months. And the total interest cost was slashed to $101,987.79 from $209,569.28. Not bad, considering that Darryl and Michelle did nothing more than apply their 5% annual raise towards the mortgage! A nominal increase in the monthly payment resulted in sizable savings.

Mark and Lee approached their increase in mortgage payment differently. Originally they booked the same mortgage as Darryl and Michelle. Knowing that most of the interest was paid in the early years of the mortgage, and that small prepayments during those early years would result in a large interest saving, they decided to permanently increase the mortgage payment by 10% effective February 1, 1990, payment 13 on the schedule. From then on, their monthly payment would be $1,135.09 instead of $1,031.90. And that's the only thing Mark and Lee ever did towards prepaying the mortgage. Were the savings worth the effort? Absolutely. The total time required to pay off the loan fell from 25 years to 17 years six months, while the total interest cost was cut from $209,569.28 to $136,989.61. Remember, all this was accomplished by permanently increasing the mortgage payment by 10% once, at the end of the first year, and nothing more!

QUESTIONS AND ANSWERS ON
INCREASING YOUR MORTGAGE PAYMENT

When shopping for the perfect mortgage and the right to increase the mortgage payment, what questions should be asked? First and foremost, be absolutely certain the "step-up" privilege appears right in the mortgage. Being told it's the lender's policy to permit increased payments over time is not good enough. Policy is subject to change; a written commitment is not.

Does the borrower face any costs if the payment is increased?
Only a few lenders levy a charge if borrowers exercise the option, but some demand that ever-present "administrative fee" for having a mortgage amending agreement signed. Be sure to check this out.

When can the payment be increased?
For ease of calculation, generally it is limited to a payment date. Mid-month hikes in payments make it very difficult to properly allocate the increase towards principal and interest.

How is the mortgage payment permanently increased?
Usually nothing more is needed than a letter from the borrower asking for it. Sometimes a certain amount of written notice must be given before the change takes effect. And without exception, lenders will only allow borrowers to increase the payment if they are up-to-date in their mortgage payments. But these are simple conditions to comply with.

How often can the payment be boosted?
Usually only once a year, at any time during the year. Again, this begs the question, as with lump-sum prepayment privileges: is that a mortgage year or calendar year? Danny and Marilyn booked their three-year mortgage on June 1, 1989. A mortgage-year option would give them three chances of increasing their payment—once from June 1, 1989, to May 31, 1990; once from June 1, 1990, to May 31, 1991; and finally once from June 1, 1991, to May 31, 1992. If Danny and Marilyn could increase their payment once each calendar year, they would have *four* opportunities during the three-year term—once in 1989, once in 1990, once in 1991, and once in 1992 before maturity.

What is the 10% (or 15%) annual increase in payment based on?
Some lenders consider only the original monthly payment. Dick and Jane, whose lender offered this 10% option, could only increase their $1,000 monthly payment by $100 each year. Peter and Rose benefitted from their lender basing the 10% increase on the current payment. As they paid $1,000 monthly the first year, they were able to increase their payment to $1,100 in year two, to $1,210 the third year, $1,331 the fourth year and $1,464.10 the fifth year. Dick and Jane on the other hand were limited to a maximum of $1,400 during the fifth year of the mortgage.

As with prepayment privileges, usually the right to increase the mortgage payment is noncumulative. If a borrower does not increase his or her payment by the permitted maximum in one year, the unused portion is lost forever.

Of those lenders that permit payments to be boosted, not all limit borrowers to 10% or 15% annually. Some permit borrowers like Owen and Melodye to increase their payment by as much as they like over the term of the mortgage, provided the total amount paid does not exceed 100% of the original monthly payment. What a generous privilege—with a five-year term, borrowers effectively can increase their payments by 20% annually. If Owen and Melodye's original payment was $1,000 monthly, they could permanently increase it (on a payment date) to any amount they choose, and continue increasing it to whatever figure they like, provided the amount paid monthly never exceeds $2,000!

MORE INS AND OUTS OF INCREASING THE PAYMENT

Be absolutely certain the right to increase the mortgage payment is not affected if you take advantage of any other prepayment privileges the lender offers (reducing the amortization, weekly payments and lump-sum prepayments). Virtually all lenders will let borrowers exercise more than one of these prepayment features, if they choose. This would allow them to pay the mortgage weekly, and also benefit from increasing the payment at a later time.

Keep in mind that the payment here is being increased *permanently*. This is not the same as the "double-up" feature available in the marketplace, which is a temporary, one-time increase in the mortgage payment equivalent to your current payment. With a "double-up," the original mortgage amount (say, $815) is paid in October, following the month (September) when the "double-up" payment ($1,630) was made. This chapter has focussed on increasing your payment to a new level, and keeping it there.

What if you discover, as Rob and Laura did, that you couldn't handle the permanent increase in the mortgage payment? In their case, the increase by 8% the first year from $1,000 to $1,080 was fine; but Rob and Laura found the second increase in the mortgage payment, to $1,150, too much of a strain for their budget.

Most lenders allow the payment to be reduced once each year if previously increased, provided the payment is not reduced below its original figure. Therefore, Rob and Laura's lender would have allowed them to decrease the payment from $1,150 to $1,000 (or anywhere in between), but no lower than $1,000. Now is the time to learn, before making any commitment, if the payment can be *reduced* after it has been increased, how often, and by how much. Be sure to get the answer in writing, too.

Allowing borrowers to increase their payments over time is another indication of how lenders today consider mortgages to be personalized loans. Many borrowers now can "customize" their mortgage payments, selecting an amount they feel comfortable with. Yet there is one time when borrowers can't choose their own payment—when the mortgage is originally booked! The reason for the distinction makes absolutely no sense.

A little background is needed to explain the inconsistency. Most lenders use a little book called an "amortization book" to learn what the blended mortgage payment will be—whether it's paid monthly, weekly or biweekly. Once the principal is determined and the interest rate set, lenders inevitably look at the book and note the figure for a 25-year amortization as the mortgage payment. Once selected, the figure is nonnegotiable. In Howard and Sheila's case, the $100,000, 12% mortgage amortized over 25 years meant the monthly payment was $1,031.90.

Howard and Sheila thought that was a strange figure for a payment. As they budgeted $1,050 monthly for the mortgage, they felt that would be the ideal payment. The extra $18.10 per month, according to their calculations, was a prepayment of the mortgage that would reduce the interest cost from $209,569.28 to $186,608.58 (a savings of $22,960.69). There would also be a faster payoff of the loan, with the amortization falling from

25 years to 22 years 9 months. Not bad, when all they wanted to do was round up the payment to an easy-to-remember number.

When they asked to have the initial payment set at $1,050 instead of $1,031.90, the loans officer said it was impossible, since the requested figure would affect the 25-year amortization for the loan. As they didn't offer loans with "funny" amortizations such as 22 years 9 months, the payment had to stay where it was.

Imagine how ludicrous that statement was. Howard and Sheila couldn't choose their own payment when the loan was being booked, but there would be no problem in increasing their monthly payment to $1,050 one month after completing the mortgage transaction! At that stage the lender didn't seem to worry that a personally selected payment would result in some oddball amortization. So why did their lender, like most others, insist on a payment based on a 25-year amortization when the funds were advanced? If the income qualifications continue to be satisfied, why can't borrowers like Howard and Sheila choose whatever higher monthly payment they like at the outset? There is no good reason why the monthly payment cannot be rounded up at that stage to the nearest $10, $5, or even $1. Why couldn't Howard and Sheila do at the beginning what they could later on, by choosing their own mortgage payment?

This is the problem with our financial institutions—they are slaves to the figures in the amortization book to the detriment of Canadian borrowers. Loans officers constantly treat the numbers in that book with the sanctity and reverence of the Bible! The figures appearing in the amortization book should never be viewed as the last step in determining what the borrower should pay. Instead, they should only be a first step—the minimum payment permitted—in determining what the payment should be. The approach taken by Howard and Sheila's lender, and by virtually all lenders, just isn't good enough.

The better way would permit borrowers to round up their own payment *at the outset*. Once the necessary qualifications have been satisfied and a tentative minimum payment calculated, based on the information in the amortization book, lenders would throw away the book. As a minimum, the payment would be rounded up to the nearest $10 or $5, whatever the borrower wanted. If the borrower said nothing, the payment would be rounded up to the nearest dollar. As higher payments reduce the amortization for the loan, all additional money paid this way would go directly to the principal, resulting in even further savings. It would also make life somewhat easier in writing post-dated cheques or processing preauthorized debit slips.

When considering rounding, never round down even a cent. It will cost borrowers extra money in the long run by extending the amortization for the loan. For example, if Howard and Sheila's payment was reduced to $1,030, the mortgage would cost them an extra $2,890 and take almost four more months to pay off.

Rounding up the mortgage payment is not the final answer, either. The best solution would allow borrowers to select their own payment *at the outset*, just as Howard and Sheila wanted to do, and not force them to wait until the mortgage was in place before granting them this privilege. Of course, this assumes the income criteria continues to be satisfied. Howard and Sheila then could tailor the payment to their ability to pay the loan. As for what the resulting amortization might be—who really cares? It certainly will be less than 25 years.

In the usual case, selecting an amortization period determines the amount of the payment. Why can't the reverse hold true, so that borrowers select a payment they can afford and want to pay, which then determines the amortization for the loan? Any other approach leaves mortgage lenders at the mercy of the AM book.

Practically speaking, some lenders do round up the payment to the nearest dollar when the mortgage is booked. But few allow the payment to be rounded to anything higher. And almost no lenders, even those that allow later increases in the mortgage payment, permit borrowers to choose their own payment at the outset. Why not is one of the great unsolved mysteries in Canada today.

Increasing the mortgage payment over time is an effective way for Canadian borrowers to pay off their principal sooner, and pare down the high cost of mortgage financing. Rounding up the payment at the beginning, and choosing your own mortgage payment at the outset, are important features to consider when shopping for a mortgage. But having the right to permanently boost your payment whenever *you* want is an essential feature of the perfect mortgage, and one that should be exercised whenever possible.

When Shopping for the Perfect Mortgage, Ask:

1) Does the right to increase the mortgage payment appear in the mortgage?
2) Is there any fee if the payment is increased?
3) Can the payment only be increased on a payment date?
4) What must be done before the payment can be increased?
5) Can the payment be boosted only once a year? Is that a mortgage year or a calendar year?
6) What is the increase in payment based on—the original payment or the current payment?
7) By how much can the payment be boosted? 10% annually? 15% annually? By up to 100% of the original payment over the life of the mortgage?
8) Is the right to increase the mortgage payment affected if you take advantage of any other prepayment privileges the lender offers?
9) Can the payment be reduced after it has been increased? On what terms?
10) Will the lender permit a rounding up of the payment at the beginning to the nearest $1; $5; $10?
11) Can you choose your own mortgage payment at the outset?

11
Paying Your Mortgage Weekly or Biweekly

Simply divide by four or two to save money

So far we have examined three of the four ways to pay off your principal sooner: lump-sum prepayments, reducing the amortization and increasing the mortgage payment. Now comes the fourth and most fascinating approach to prepaying your mortgage.

Instead of paying the mortgage monthly, why not pay it weekly or biweekly (every two weeks)? What an interesting idea! Just because the time-honoured tradition has been monthly payments, there's no magic in that. Most people receive their salary every week, every two weeks or twice a month. Wouldn't it be more convenient to pay the mortgage every week, two weeks or twice a month as well? This would assist family budgeting, by allowing borrowers to co-ordinate their mortgage payment dates to their salary pay days. So far it sounds great. But now comes the all-important question: will it save borrowers money? *Will it save borrowers money*? Yes, yes, yes, tens of thousands of dollars.

For simplicity, we'll refer to fast-pay mortgages (weekly, biweekly and semi-monthly) as just weekly mortgages. And despite its critics, they are the easiest and most effective way to dramatically reduce the long-term interest cost of Canadian residential mortgages! Like most of the features making up the perfect mortgage, some lenders offer weekly mortgages, some don't. It's availability depends on the individual lender. But there are also a few booby traps to be wary of, pitfalls that could destroy its usefulness and potential.

Weekly mortgages are not a gimmick or a "scheme." Unlike some ideas that are borderline legal, fast-pay mortgages increase the number of times the mortgage is paid each year. No more, no less. It changes the one feature of mortgage financing that has remained untouched until now—how often it is paid. Because the benefits make the plan appear too good to be true, and the approach seems peculiar at first, people assume there has to be "a catch." There isn't.

How can a borrower decide if a weekly-payment mortgage is right for him or her? Ask yourself the following question: if the blended payment of principal and interest was $400 per month, are you prepared to pay one-quarter of this amount (or $100) every week, or one-half of that amount (or $200) every two weeks instead? If the answer is yes, you are a prime candidate for a fast-pay mortgage. It's as straightforward as that.

Peter and Lydia originally were going to arrange the $100,000, 12% mortgage that appears on page 135. Amortized over 25 years, the monthly payment is $1,031.90. The total interest cost for this loan over those 25 years: $209,569.28. It is the mortgage shown on line I on the chart that appears on page 61, and is the yardstick against which the fast-pay mortgage must be compared.

What if Peter and Lydia decided to pay their mortgage weekly? Instead of paying $1,031.90 each month, they would pay one-quarter of that, or $257.98 each week. The results of increasing the frequency of their mortgage payments, converting the monthly pay mortgage into a weekly-pay mortgage, appears in line II.

The numbers are astounding. Simply by paying one-quarter of the normal monthly payment each week (while everything else stays the same), Peter and Lydia will pare down over 30% of the total time needed to fully pay off this mortgage—to around 17 years four months. The amount of nondeductible interest they save by doing nothing more than dividing by four and paying that amount weekly: over $76,000! Remember that all this is achieved by paying one-quarter of the normal monthly payment each week, without any change in the interest rate or the manner in which the interest is calculated. Amazing!

The savings are nearly as substantial if one-half of the normal monthly payment is made every two weeks, as shown in line III. The payoff time is just slightly higher, and the total interest saved is just slightly lower. But neither difference is significant. Therefore, if you are paid every two weeks, it's not worth going to the trouble of paying your mortgage weekly. Matching your mortgage payment to your pay day, and paying the lender bi-weekly, will do just fine.

How do weekly mortgages work? Why does a simple shift in payments result in such enormous savings for borrowers? The

Comparative Table	Payments	Amortized Life of Loan	Total Interest Cost for Loan	Interest Saved Over Conventional Loan (I)	Extra Amount Paid Annually
I. Conventional monthly payment	$1,031.90	25 years	$209,569.28	N/A	N/A
II. Monthly amount paid in four weekly instalments	$257.98	17.38 years	$133,141.04	$76,428.24	$1,032.16
III. Monthly amount paid in two biweekly instalments	$515.95	17.44 years	$133,988.27	$75,581.61	$1,031.90
IV. Annual amount paid in 52 weekly instalments	$238.13	24.15 years	$199,050.00	$10,519.28	NIL
V. Annual amount paid in 26 biweekly instalments	$476.26	24.30 years	$200,920.53	$8,648.75	NIL

answer is twofold; the first reason is the "accelerated reduction of principal." More payments are being made (52 instead of 12) each year to the lender. Therefore the outstanding principal is being reduced faster than normal. It is similar to depositing money in a bank. If you put $1 in a daily-interest savings account at the end of each week, you'll have more money in the account at the end of four weeks than if you put $4 in the account at the end of the fourth week. The more often you pay, the greater the compounding effect.

While the additional number of payments made annually results in some interest savings, its impact is small compared to reason number two: the "built-in prepayment of principal" that weekly mortgages provide. While there are 12 months in a year, there are also 13 "four-week" periods. With a blended payment of $400 per month, $4,800 would be paid to the lender annually. With a blended payment of $100 per week (or $200 every two weeks), $5,200 would be paid to the lender by the end of the year. In other words, borrowers effectively prepay the equivalent of one extra mortgage payment to the lender annually with a weekly mortgage. The last column of lines II and III clearly shows this. The entire additional amount prepaid each year goes directly to reduce the outstanding principal on the loan.

BEWARE OF TRAPS!

Be careful. Not all lenders take the same approach to weekly payments. The proper way to calculate a weekly mortgage payment appears in lines II and III. Here, the regular *monthly* amount is divided by four for weekly payments, or by two for biweekly payments. Other lenders bastardize the idea by taking the total *annual* amount paid on the mortgage, and dividing it by 52 for weekly payments (or 26 for biweekly payments). Then they deceive an unsuspecting public into believing this is the "real" weekly mortgage. It isn't.

Paying the annual amount of principal and interest more frequently than monthly results in only a nominal saving in interest costs, and a negligible effect in reducing the amortization for the loan. Consider again the example of the $400 blended monthly mortgage payment. If the weekly payment was 1/52nd of the total annual payment, the weekly payment would be $400 times 12, or $4,800, divided by 52, or $92.31 instead of $100. On a biweekly basis the payment would be $184.62 instead of $200. The only benefit to borrowers is the "accelerated reduction of principal." The missing $7.69 paid weekly (or $15.38 paid every two weeks) is the "built-in prepayment of principal" borrowers want with the real fast-pay plan, the amount that makes the idea work. While this doesn't seem like much of a difference, its impact is phenomenal.

Lines IV and V on the chart clearly show this. Remember that at all times the interest rate is 12% calculated semi-annually, not in advance. If Peter and Lydia paid the annual amount in 52 weekly instalments, the "accelerated reduction of principal" would save them about 10 months' worth of mortgage payments and over $10,000 in interest costs. But as the last column indicates, the built-in prepayment of principal of a true fast-pay mortgage is missing. If the same annual amount was paid in 26 biweekly instalments, the "accelerated reduction of principal" would save them eight months worth of mortgage payments and over $8,500 in interest costs. Once again, there is no built-in prepayment of principal as with a genuine biweekly mortgage. To benefit from fast-pay mortgages, the monthly payment rather than the annual payment must be used.

It's not necessary to be a mathematician, economist or financial wizard to benefit from weekly mortgages. All you need to do is divide the conventional monthly payment by two or four and pay that amount biweekly or monthly. This will automatically reduce the interest cost of a mortgage, and the time needed to fully retire the loan, by 30% or more at no extra cost!

There's no question that most of the savings result from paying more towards the mortgage each year than from the increased number of payments. There is also no question that a similar result in the weekly mortgage plan could be achieved by prepaying one extra mortgage payment each year. But that is not the point. While many people want to prepay their mortgages, they find it difficult to save a lump sum of money each year. By contrast the built-in prepayment of a weekly mortgage makes it easy to pay off the principal sooner. After all, a small amount of money (1/52nd or 1/26th of an additional payment) is prepaid with each payment. Simplicity is its greatest virtue.

Amortization schedules can easily be ordered showing the proper breakdown of weekly/biweekly payments between principal and interest. Computer programs are readily available that analyze the benefits of paying more often than monthly. They reflect a growing acceptance of the concept in the mainstream of mortgage financing.

Be on the lookout for several other potential traps when booking a weekly mortgage. Make sure the interest rate is the same whether you pay the loan monthly or sooner. Paying even one-quarter of one per cent more for the privilege of a fast-pay mortgage reduces its effectiveness. Also be certain the loan continues to be calculated semi-annually, not in advance. A shift towards calculating the loan monthly, biweekly or even weekly will cost the borrower money.

When inquiring about fast-pay mortgages, ask when the payments must be made. Most lenders insist that weekly mortgages be paid every Friday, and biweekly payments every second Friday. But other lenders will collect their payments any weekday.

Be sure the right to pay weekly exists independently of any other prepayment privileges the lender may have. In other words, make absolutely certain that although the mortgage is paid weekly, you still can take advantage of other important prepayment privileges the lender may offer (reducing the amortization, increasing the payment, lump-sum prepayments). Also see if there is any fee for a weekly mortgage. Usually there isn't, if the weekly arrangement is sought when the mortgage is arranged or on a renewal. But converting from a monthly-pay mortgage to a weekly mortgage in mid-term could mean the borrower must pay that ever-present administrative fee.

After booking a weekly mortgage, Buddy and Sally discovered that it just wasn't for them. Thankfully they inquired, and received written assurance from their lender before signing the mortgage commitment that it could be converted back to a monthly-pay mortgage. The only restriction was that the payment could be no lower than it would be with a 25-year amortization. This is why their lender registered the mortgage on title as a conventional monthly-payment mortgage, the weekly option appearing in a side agreement. To revert to a monthly payment, all Buddy and Sally have to do is cancel the side agreement.

The Canadian public today sees weekly mortgages as an innovative answer to the problems of high interest rates, large mortgage payments and sizable interest costs. An ever-increasing number of institutional lenders now offer fast-pay mortgages—a signal that the voice of Canadians for better mortgages is being heard. More and more American borrowers, with mortgage interest deductibility, are flocking to the fast-pay plan. Since we in Canada generally can't do the same, isn't that all the more reason to consider paying our mortgages more often than monthly?

Weekly mortgage payments are an important feature of the perfect mortgage. Even if you can't take full advantage of the plan today, it's a nice option to have available for tomorrow. But remember that a genuine weekly mortgage is based on one-quarter of the monthly payment. Accept no substitutes.

When Shopping for the Perfect Mortgage, Ask:

1) Will the lender allow weekly or biweekly payments?
2) Is the weekly payment one-quarter of the regular monthly payment (one-half for biweekly payments)? Avoid mortgages where the weekly payment is 1/52 of the regular annual payment (1/26 for biweekly payments).
3) What day of the week will the payments be made?
4) Is the interest rate the same for a weekly mortgage? Is the interest still calculated semi-annually, not in advance?
5) Can you still take advantage of the lender's other prepayment features if you pay your mortgage weekly?
6) Can the mortgage be converted back to a monthly-pay mortgage? If so, on what terms?

12
Interest Rate Differentials

How all mortgages could be 100% open

Would you like to be able to totally pay off your mortgage whenever *you* want? That's right, the borrower and not the lender would decide when it could be prepaid.

What if you could pay off as much or as little principal as *you* chose each year? That's quite a departure from today, where most institutional lenders restrict you to an annual limit of 10% or 15% of the amount originally borrowed.

Would you be in favour of a penalty for early prepayment that was fair and reasonable, instead of one that was arbitrary and often meaningless? Not only that, but some borrowers might be able to fully pay off their mortgages without incurring any penalty, perhaps even getting a reduction on what is owed!

These are not the whimsical desires of a crazed borrower. Instead they describe a new and exciting way to prepay mortgages *now available* from lenders across Canada. The name for this idea is present value prepayments or, as it is now being called, the "interest rate differential" or IRD approach in determining the prepayment penalty. The essence of the scheme is simple: if a mortgage is paid off early, the lender will be fully, fairly and adequately compensated *only* for the lost interest resulting from the prepayment—no more and no less. Using the IRD, all Canadians could benefit from paying off the outstanding principal as quickly as possible, both on a sale of the property, or if the borrower simply wants to retire the loan.

Having the IRD as the prepayment penalty is one of the most important features of the perfect mortgage. But borrowers shopping for a mortgage must remember that not all institutional lenders offer the IRD. Of those that do, many tamper with the concept, destroying its effectiveness. The IRD is such a pivotal ingredient to the perfect mortgage that it could be *the* distinguishing factor why one lender's package is selected over another's, when all other features are equal.

Under basic contract law, if one party breaches a contract the other party is entitled to be put in the same position as it would have been in had there been no breach. As a prepayment of the mortgage is equivalent to a breach of that contract, when a mortgage is prepaid borrowers must adequately compensate lenders for their losses by putting the lender in the same position as it would have been in had there been no breach.

Unfortunately, ordinary contract concepts and remedies did not apply to prepayments of mortgages until now. This explains why residential Canadian mortgages are fully closed, why borrowers have no right to prepay their mortgages, and why lenders can exact whatever penalty they want when a prepayment is made—unless a prepayment privilege appears right in the mortgage.

Where the IRD approach is used, the prepayment penalty charged is not some arbitrary and irrelevant figure such as three months' interest penalty. Instead, the penalty paid properly reflects the true cost to the lender of the prepayment—taking in the money from one borrower, and relending it to another.

The interest rate differential is a formula that looks at the "present value" (a concept discussed below) of the difference in the interest rates (contractual vs. current) on the outstanding principal for the balance of the mortgage term. A prepayment penalty based on the interest rate differential gives lenders their just due, without creating any windfall profits.

Simply put, the interest rate differential places the lender in the same position as it would have been in had there been no breach (no prepayment). With the IRD, all mortgages would now be in category 2 discussed in Chapter 8, 100% open with a predetermined penalty. Besides eliminating the confusion about open and fully open mortgages, there would be no need to negotiate a penalty, cap-in-hand, with the lender when the mortgage is to be paid off before it matures. To learn what it will cost to cancel a mortgage, simply plug the numbers into the formula at the appropriate time. Adoption of the IRD approach to prepaying mortgages would level the inequality of bargaining power that currently exists between lenders and borrowers.

To understand how interest rate differentials work, let's examine the $100,000, 12%, category 3 "limited open" mortgage Alan and Hannah arranged three years ago that appears on page 135. Booked for a five-year term, the monthly payments amortized over 25 years were $1,031.90. The present balance on their mortgage after three years is $97,597.48.

Having sold their home, Alan and Hannah now want to fully pay off the loan. If they were charged a penalty of three months' interest, Alan and Hannah would have to pay a penalty of $2,857.29 (the interest component in payment 37 of $952.43 times three) to discharge their mortgage. But this penalty really is meaningless; it does not reflect the cost of the prepayment to the lender or what it will cost to take in the money before the mortgage matures and to put it back "out on the street."

What the arbitrary three months penalty doesn't do, the IRD approach does. When Alan and Hannah decided to prepay their mortgage, interest rates had fallen—the current rate for two-year mortgages (the time remaining on their mortgage) was 11%. If the prepayment penalty were based on the IRD, a fair penalty reflecting the cost to the lender of taking back the money would appear to be 1% (12% less 11%) multiplied by $97,597.48 multiplied by two (for two years still outstanding), for a total of $1,951.95. In other words, it would appear that a lump-sum payment of that amount would put the lender in the same position it would have been in had there been no prepayment. But that figure only considered the 1% difference in the actual interest rates. Even that penalty would put more money in the lender's pocket than it deserves. How and why?

If Alan and Hannah didn't prepay their mortgage now, that $1,951.95 would go to the lender little by little over the next 24 months. With the $1,951.95 loss of interest differential being paid "up front," the lender can invest it at 11% over the next two years to generate even more interest. To be fair to Alan and Hannah and eliminate a windfall for the lender, the "raw" number of $1,951.95 must be reduced to reflect this. That's why to properly calculate the IRD, the *present value* of the difference in the interest rates must be examined, not just the difference in the rates themselves. This is a key distinction.

What is this present value in the difference in interest rates? How is it calculated? What is the exact penalty Alan and Hannah must pay to prepay their mortgage using the IRD? First, as the final figure itself will generate some interest, it obviously must be less than the "raw" number of $1,951.95, although it gives Alan and Hannah a rough idea of the maximum penalty.

What they are looking for is the number that will produce

$1,951.95 when invested at 11% for two years. At the same time Alan and Hannah also must take into account the different mortgage payments during that period at interest rates of 12% and 11%, plus the slightly different balances that will be outstanding when both loans mature.

While the exact mathematical calculations may be complex, a mortgage discount table or computer program can calculate the precise penalty in seconds. Looking at Alan and Hannah's situation, the penalty based on the IRD would be $1,653.47. This is the figure that accurately and fairly compensates the lender for the lost interest over the remaining two years if Alan and Hannah pay off their mortgage now. Prepayment of the outstanding principal plus payment of this amount now would put the lender in exactly the same position at the end of two years as it would have been in had there been no prepayment. Any penalty here greater than $1,653.47 would be unjustified.

Who can benefit from interest rate differentials? *Everyone.* On a sale, borrowers can immediately determine what the prepayment penalty will be if the mortgage must be paid off. With a prepayment penalty based on the IRD, it is much easier to renew a mortgage before maturity, "locking-in" for a long term when interest rates are low. The same is true if you just want to reduce the amount owing on the mortgage. In all these cases the penalty paid will recognize the true cost of the prepayment to the lender.

There are three possible scenarios concerning interest rates if the IRD is used to determine a prepayment penalty: a) current rates could be lower (as we have seen); b) they could be the same; or c) they could be higher than the rate stated in the mortgage. Regardless of the circumstances, the results are interesting. Scenario 2 is stable interest rates. Assume they were the same (12%) when Alan and Hannah wanted to prepay their mortgage as when they booked it. Once again, three years had passed on the five-year mortgage shown on page 135. What would the penalty be (ignoring transaction costs), following the IRD approach? *Nothing!* That's right. *Absolutely nothing.* In raw numbers it would be 0% multiplied by $97,597.48 multiplied by two years, or $0.00. If rates are the same, being able to prepay this mortgage without incurring any penalty makes a lot of sense. After all, the lender could take back Alan and Hannah's 12% mortgage money and put it out on the street at the same rate. Net cost to the lender? Nil. Charging a three months' interest penalty looks quite arbitrary in this situation.

Now let's examine scenario 3, the reverse of scenario 1. Assume interest rates have gone up since Alan and Hannah booked their mortgage. A two-year mortgage now costs 13% when they decide to prepay their 12% loan. What then? Instead of receiving 12% over the next two years, their lender could earn another 1% (13% less 12%) for two years if Alan and Hannah paid off their mortgage now. In raw numbers the interest generated would be 1% on $97,597.48 multiplied by two years, or $1,951.94. Precisely calculated, the bonus being earned is $1,616.22.

Since Alan and Hannah had to pay a penalty to prepay their mortgage when rates fell from 12% to 11%, to be fair shouldn't they *receive* an IRD rebate or bonus *from the lender* if rates had increased from 12% to 13% when the mortgage was prepaid? In theory, yes, but practically speaking, not yet.

The underlying principle behind the IRD is that the lender be in the same position as it would have been in had there been no prepayment. If it keeps the bonus when rates have gone up, as is almost always the case, Alan and Hannah are penalized while the lender reaps an unjustified profit. After all, if it's sauce for the goose it should be sauce for the gander. Alan and Hannah are doing their lender a favour by repaying their 12% mortgage, when the lender can earn a higher rate of interest by relending the money. If the IRD concept applies when rates fall, it should apply equally when rates rise, but in reverse. Maybe someday. . . .

Even if no rebate is paid when current mortgage rates are higher than the contractual rate of interest, certainly the lender should not charge any prepayment penalty. Charging Alan and Hannah a three months' penalty in these circumstances would be even more unjust. It would defeat the entire purpose of the IRD—a penalty that reflects the true cost to the lender of accepting a premature retirement of the loan.

Unknown to most people, in 1984 the IRD came within a whisker of being the law of the land. That year the federal government made a very bold but simple comment in its budget, saying "all Canadians should have the right to prepay their mortgages. When they do so, however, lenders should be compensated for the losses incurred." To guard against exorbitant penalties and windfall profits, "the maximum prepayment penalty should be the present value of the difference, over the balance of the mortgage term, between the interest stream at the currently prevailing market interest rates and the interest stream at the rate provided for in the mortgage being repaid"—what it calls "the present value of the loss incurred," or the IRD. This would "give borrowers the right to prepay their mortgages at any time." Draft legislation on the topic was introduced in the House of Commons in 1984 but died on the Order Paper.

In a major study of mortgages, the Ontario Law Reform Commission (OLRC) in 1987 said that residential borrowers "should be entitled to prepay the loan at any time, provided the lender is fully compensated for the actual loss incurred as a result of the prepayment. . . . The formula for determining the value of the prepayment compensation to the lender would be the present value of the difference between the amount that the lender would have earned under the security agreement, and the amount that, at current market rates of interest, the lender would now earn in a substitute investment." Once again, it's the IRD.

Surprisingly, neither study discussed the possibility of interest rates being higher at the time of prepayment, entitling borrowers to a rebate of money in these circumstances. The draft 1984 legislation was silent on the point as well. Understandably, institutional lenders are also very reluctant to discuss this issue. While it is clear what should be done, what will actually happen is anybody's guess.

Both the federal budget and the OLRC acknowledged that reasonable administrative fees or "transaction costs" would also have to be levied if mortgages were prepaid using the IRD, to cover taking in the money, holding it, and lending it back out at current rates. The budget anticipated what it called "mortgage initiation fees," while the OLRC took a more practical approach: "in addition to prepayment compensation, a lender should be entitled to compensation for the administrative fees in relending the money," not to exceed one month's interest.

How receptive have the major financial institutions been to this idea, considering how it threatens to eliminate a major source of revenue? In the last few years, as a direct response to the extremely competitive residential mortgage market, a handful of major institutional lenders have adopted "modified" versions of the IRD scheme. But no one has adopted the concept in its purest form, applying it to all lump-sum prepayments.

One institutional lender has adopted the IRD as its prepayment penalty, tacking on as well an administrative charge of $500 that is paid when the prepayment is made. This fee, which is reduced by $100 each year, approximates the "transaction costs" both the federal budget and the OLRC addressed. However, it doesn't offer a rebate or bonus if rates rise.

Be careful of several other lenders that have adopted a bastardized version of the IRD—a prepayment penalty consisting of the *greater* of three months' bonus interest or the IRD. If the IRD represents the true cost to the lender over the balance of the mortgage term of taking the money in early and relending it, a penalty based on the IRD should suffice. In most cases, though, borrowers will still be paying the arbitrary three months' penalty. Talk about having it both ways!

- If the mortgage rate was the same as the current interest rate, the IRD would be 0. The borrower would then have to pay three months' penalty.
- If the mortgage rate was less than the current interest rate (i.e. rates had risen), the IRD would be 0 (actually it would be a negative figure). Once again, the borrower would have to pay three months' penalty.
- If the mortgage rate was higher than the current interest rate (i.e. rates had fallen), the penalty could be either the IRD or the three months' penalty, depending on the outstanding term of the mortgage and the difference in the rates. Interest rates must have fallen considerably, though, before the IRD penalty exceeded the three months' interest penalty.

And, be especially wary of the odd lender that charges *both* the IRD and three months' bonus interest as the penalty!

While no one is prepared to pay a bonus if interest rates are higher when the mortgage is prepaid, one major institutional lender at least addresses the issue. Unfortunately, the response is anything but adequate. If interest rates at the time of the prepayment are 2% or more above the mortgage interest rate, no prepayment penalty is charged (but it won't give you the rebate either). If the rate increase is less than 2% since the mortgage was booked, the penalty charged is the greater of the IRD and three months' bonus penalty. Since the IRD only imposes a penalty when rates have dropped, borrowers in this situation still have to pay a three months' interest penalty. Despite its initial allure, this lender is being far from charitable. Still, it recognizes the fact that charging penalties when rates go up and mortgages are prepaid is a windfall to the lender.

Other lenders use the interest rate differential in one limited situation only—when calculating the penalty charged to borrowers invoking the "early renewal" clause offered in some mortgages (discussed in Chapter 16). The irony of it all. To *renew* the mortgage before it matures, the "charge" is the present value in the difference in the interest rates, on the outstanding principal, for the remainder of the mortgage term. But these same lenders won't adopt the IRD approach when a borrower wants to *pay off* a mortgage early instead of renewing it! Since they have already adopted the idea for early renewals, why don't they extend its application to include all prepayments? Still, this is a strong indication of the slow acceptance the IRD is gaining in Canada today.

Interest rate differentials do not eliminate prepayment penalties for all borrowers. Just as in a popular TV commercial, "You can pay me now or pay me later." When the IRD is applied, borrowers effectively still pay the contractual mortgage interest rate for the rest of the mortgage term. However, instead of paying the higher interest rate on the outstanding principal over time until the mortgage matures, the IRD allows borrowers to pay the difference in the interest rates up front when the prepayment is made. If rates are stable or have increased, borrowers should be able to eliminate the penalty altogether. But the most important feature of the IRD is the way it eliminates arbitrary penalties and windfall profits. It brings an equality of bargaining power to the borrower/lender relationship that otherwise wouldn't exist.

Despite its apparent attractiveness to borrowers and the positive steps taken by lenders, it's naive to believe all lenders will voluntarily adopt the IRD as the accepted prepayment penalty for residential mortgages. In recent years the banking industry has come under increasing criticism about its "service charges." The exorbitant profits being made from unwarranted, arbitrary prepayment penalties makes the concern about bank service charges look pale by comparison.

Strong, courageous action by our politicians (whether provincial or federal is an interesting legal issue) is needed to ensure that homeowners can pay off their mortgages whenever *they* want, without penalizing lenders. Legislating the interest rate differential into existence won't cost government any money. But it will deny money to lenders that they aren't entitled to.

Until the law changes, one of the key features to consider when shopping for the perfect mortgage is whether the lender uses the interest rate differential as its prepayment penalty. Some do, most don't; it depends on the lender. Mortgages are readily available today in the Canadian marketplace from lenders using the IRD. It's a question of seeking them out.

When Shopping for the Perfect Mortgage, Ask:

1) Does the lender apply the interest rate differential approach to prepayment penalties—the present value of the difference in the interest rates (contractual vs. current) on the outstanding principal for the balance of the mortgage term?
2) Does the lender apply a modified form of the IRD (i.e. the greater of three months' interest penalty or the interest rate differential, or perhaps three months' interest penalty and the interest rate differential)?
3) Does the lender charge any administrative fee in addition to the IRD?
4) If mortgage rates at the time of the prepayment are higher than the contract rate, does the lender offer a rebate?

13
Property Tax Accounts

Convenient or costly?

Property taxes—everyone knows they have to be paid. With a mortgage-free house, you pay the taxes directly to the municipality. But that's not necessarily the case once you borrow money on a mortgage. When, how and who pays the property taxes could depend on the type of tax clause in your mortgage.

Many mortgage lenders insist that borrowers pay part of the estimated annual property taxes *to the lender* with each regular mortgage payment (one-twelfth if the mortgage is paid monthly, or the appropriate percentage if payments are made weekly, biweekly or semi-monthly). Funds collected by the lender this way are placed into a "property tax" or "escrow" account. Tax bills are sent directly to the lender, which pays the taxes for the borrower from this account when they are due.

Why are lenders so concerned about property taxes that they act as middlemen? According to provincial law, unpaid taxes are a "super" lien against a property, ranking even higher than a first mortgage. By collecting part of the taxes with each mortgage payment, lenders never have to worry about losing their priority status.

In trying to sell homeowners/borrowers on the merits of tax accounts, lenders emphasize their convenience. By combining the mortgage and taxes into one payment, borrowers don't face a sizable lump-sum outlay when a tax instalment is due. This is supposed to help homeowners with their budgeting.

Like most conveniences, this one costs borrowers money. It can also have a serious impact on personal budgeting. That's why borrowers shopping for the perfect mortgage should try to pay their property taxes directly to the municipality, rather than indirectly through the mortgage lender. Since not all lenders operate them, a key feature to consider when shopping for a mortgage is the property tax account.

A tax account can devastate a borrower's cash flow, both when refinancing an existing mortgage or when arranging a new mortgage for a home purchase. Homeowners with tax accounts in their mortgages usually prepay their property taxes up to six months in advance! In the typical situation, borrowers must:

a) pay any previously issued but still unpaid tax bills when the mortgage funds are received, bringing the current taxes up-to-date;

b) make a lump-sum "initial contribution" to set up the tax account when the mortgage funds are received; and

c) pay the "tax component" with each regular mortgage payment. This estimated figure is subject to change when property taxes increase.

From a lender's point of view, the prepayment of property taxes makes sense. Tax bills are issued twice a year. In order to have enough money on hand to honour the next bill, lenders must collect money for taxes up to six months ahead of time. But when borrowers appreciate the consequences, it's very difficult to accept paying up to half of next year's taxes this year.

George and Rochelle closed their home purchase in early June 1989. The annual taxes on the house were $1,800. Since their lender, Mountie Bank, operated a property tax account, on closing George and Rochelle had to pay the unpaid balance of the 1989 tax bill in the amount of $1,000 (a).

To establish the account, Mountie Bank also insisted on a $200 initial contribution (b). And to guarantee they were made, Mountie Bank took $1,200 "right off the top," deducting it at source from the mortgage advance. On closing it sent $1,000 to the municipal tax office and deposited the other $200 into the tax account. As they received $1,200 less from the mortgage advance anticipated, George and Rochelle needed an extra $1,200 to close their purchase. Besides all this, George and Rochelle still would be paying $150 each month into the tax account, starting August 1989 (c).

While the cash-flow crisis for closing was bad enough, George and Rochelle were puzzled about where the money for taxes was going. If all outstanding 1989 taxes had been paid to the municipality on closing, why was another $200 being deducted at that time? The answer: to be held by Mountie Bank and used to pay *1990* taxes! What about the $150 being paid monthly? The answer: it too would be applied towards *1990* property taxes! In other words, since all 1989 taxes had been paid on closing, both the $200 initial contribution and the $150 monthly payment effectively represented a prepayment by George and Rochelle in 1989 of their 1990 property taxes!

Recognizing the cash-flow crisis created by tax accounts, some lenders ask borrowers to pay the *next* tax bill when issued. The help it provides for closing is offset by the considerable confusion caused. Just like George and Rochelle, on closing their purchase Jeff and Joanne had to pay the balance of 1989 taxes. While they also had to pay a tax component with each mortgage instalment, Jeff and Joanne did not face the initial lump-sum contribution to establish the tax account (b). Instead, they had to pay the property taxes for the first half of 1990 directly to the municipality. The lender would start paying taxes from the tax account starting with the second half of 1990. In the long run, Jeff and Joanne found this midstream shift in payment responsibility bewildering. Either they or the lender should pay the taxes, but not both.

Other lenders take a different approach to ensure there will be enough money available to pay the tax bills when due. They eliminate the bothersome initial lump-sum contribution, and then collect 15 to 18 months' worth of taxes over the first 12 months of the mortgage term. The largest mortgage payments (for principal, interest and taxes) will be during the early months, with the payments actually falling when the tax component returns to "normal." Borrowers dislike this arrangement too, as the first series of payments (financially, the hardest to make) becomes artificially inflated.

If the lender insists on operating a tax account, make sure it maintains *separate* accounts, one for the taxes and another for the principal and interest. Occasionally a lender combines the two. Tax instalments paid are added to the amount owing on the mortgage, while tax components received are deducted from the principal. Because the outstanding balance is constantly going up and down, the amortization schedule for the mortgage becomes useless. Proper verification of the amount owing is impossible.

There is one small saving grace to property tax accounts. By their very nature, most tax accounts are always in credit balance. When the time comes to pay off the mortgage, this extra money in the tax account will reduce the amount that has to be paid to obtain a discharge. Of course if the reverse were true and the tax account was in debit balance, that figure would be added to the amount of the principal owing.

Although they had to prepay some of their 1990 taxes in 1989, George and Rochelle assumed they earned a fair rate of interest on their money in the property tax account. Incorrect. Most lenders pay no interest or an arbitrarily low figure on funds in this account, such as the 3% George and Rochelle earned. Rare is the lender who credits borrowers with a savings account rate of interest. With thousands of mortgages in their portfolios, institutional lenders earn hundreds of thousands of dollars this way each year. This free or relatively cheap source of funds is a major reason behind lenders' reluctance to permit borrowers to pay their own property taxes.

What if the current taxes exceeded the amount collected by the lender for taxes, and the tax account went into debit balance? Since they earned 3% interest on funds in the tax account, George and Rochelle assumed any shortfall would only cost 3%. Wrong again. According to their mortgage, any arrears caused by an outlay of money for taxes were considered to be money lent. The rate charged by Mountie Bank would be the mortgage interest rate—12%. How ironic that lenders don't pay borrowers the mortgage interest rate on credit balances, but charge the mortgage interest rate on debit balances!

According to provincial law, land can't be sold for overdue property taxes unless it has been in arrears a minimum number of years. (In Ontario, for example, taxes must be unpaid for at least three years). Since George and Rochelle booked a one-year mortgage, it was impossible for them to ever lose their property for nonpayment of property taxes during the term of the mortgage! Then why did Mountie Bank, and why do so many other lenders, insist on tax accounts for mortgages with terms of six months, one year, two years and even three years? Even if no taxes were ever paid, the property could never be sold for tax arrears while the mortgage is outstanding.

When asked this question, lenders argue that operating a tax account ensures the property taxes will be up-to-date when the mortgage is renewed. If that is the lenders' real concern, why can't borrowers with short-term mortgages pay their own property taxes? As a condition to renewing the mortgage, the borrower would then have to provide proof that all taxes had been paid.

George and Rochelle were also surprised that their sizable equity in the property (40% of the purchase price) made no difference to their lender. After all, the mortgage represented only 60% of the value of their home. Unfortunately they didn't know that some lenders who normally require tax accounts also have an unadvertised discretionary policy that allows borrowers to "opt out" and pay their own taxes in certain circumstances!

On request only, and usually before the commitment is signed, some (but not all) lenders will suspend the tax account if a borrower has 40% or 50% equity in the property. This power to waive the tax account is one of the few discretions institutional mortgage officers have. Few lenders will let a good quality mortgage slip away just because the borrower wants to pay his or her own taxes. If you have a good equity cushion to offer a lender, whether on a new loan or a refinancing, insist that the lender waive the requirement of a tax account. If the lender refuses, say you'll take your business elsewhere (assuming you have found another lender that offers the same overall mortgage package). And don't make it an idle threat.

The right to pay property taxes directly to the tax department should appear in the mortgage document that secures the loan. However, if your lender is waiving its usual requirement of a tax account, get *written* confirmation from the lender, usually in the form of a side agreement. Even when they pay their own taxes, most lenders require that borrowers provide them with receipted tax bills at the end of each calendar year. Lenders also reserve the right to reinstate the tax account if the borrower fails to pay the property taxes promptly when they fall due. But these are simple conditions to satisfy.

Borrowers who don't have 40% to 50% equity now need not despair. Over time they might find themselves satisfying these requirements. It might be possible to accomplish tomorrow what can't be accomplished today. Therefore, try to get a written commitment from the lender to that effect now, for future use.

Borrowers who pay their own taxes can easily duplicate the convenience of a property tax account, but without the cost. Instead of sending the tax component to the lender with each mortgage payment, David and Susan set up a separate daily-interest savings account. When each mortgage payment fell due, they deposited the amount of the would-be tax component into the account. This was done regularly, and without fail. Over time the account had the same amount of money in it as the lenders' tax account, while earning David and Susan a fair rate of interest. And they, not the lender, were in control of the funds at all times. Each time a tax bill was issued, it could easily be paid without any impact on their financial resources.

Not all lenders require property tax accounts. Some do, some don't: it depends on the individual lender. Some institutional lenders and virtually all private lenders have nothing to do with them. Their business is lending money, not administering tax payments. To these lenders, if you are mature enough to borrow their money, you are mature enough to pay your own taxes. The irony of it all—some lenders entrust borrowers with hundreds of thousands of dollars of mortgage money, yet they feel insecure about those same borrowers paying a fraction of that amount to the tax office each year!

While property taxes are a legitimate charge all borrowers face, having to pay them to the lender with each mortgage payment can lead to a serious cash-flow problem. With the perfect mortgage, borrowers would pay their own property taxes. Using the language of the industry, borrowers are better off paying just "P and I" (principal and interest) each month or week, instead of "PIT" (principal, interest and taxes). When it comes to property tax accounts, convenience is costly. The right to pay property taxes directly could be *the* factor that makes you choose one lender's package over another.

When Shopping for the Perfect Mortgage, Ask:

1) Can I pay my property taxes myself, or must I pay money with each mortgage instalment into a separate property tax account maintained by the lender?

2) Is interest paid on money in the account? If so, at what rate?

3) What interest rate do I pay if the account goes into debit balance?

4) How much do I have to pay to bring the current taxes up-to-date? as a lump-sum "initial contribution" setting up the tax account? as the "tax component" with each regular mortgage payment?

14
Due-On-Sale Clauses

Can a purchaser assume my mortgage?

Not everybody owns a property until the mortgage matures. Many people sell their homes during the term of the mortgage. This chapter examines clauses in current use, outlining what happens to the mortgage if the property is sold midterm.

When selling their house with an outstanding mortgage, Michael and Susan face three distinct possibilities:

a) the buyer (Andy) wants the mortgage: he will assume or "take over" the mortgage, and become responsible for paying the mortgage in the future; here Andy pays "cash to the mortgage," the cash plus the mortgage assumed equalling the purchase price;

b) Michael and Susan as sellers want the mortgage: they will take it to the new house being bought; or

c) neither the buyer nor the seller wants the mortgage: from Andy's perspective the outstanding principal could be too small, it could be too large, the interest rate could be higher than the current "going" rate, Andy might be arranging a company or family loan or he might want to pay all cash. From Michael and Susan's viewpoint they are not buying another house, or they are "trading down"—buying a smaller house and no longer need a mortgage.

The solution to (b) is the portable mortgage, discussed in Chapter 15, while Chapter 8 dealing with prepayment privileges examines the answer to (c). This chapter will review (a), and in particular this question: Is the mortgage assumable by a purchaser of the property if it is sold?

Too often this question is wrongly phrased: "Is the mortgage transferable?" Transferring a mortgage is a lender's concern, as it may want to sell the mortgage and get the money back before the mortgage matures. When a buyer wants to take over responsibility for paying the mortgage, the question is properly one of "assumability," not transferability.

Why do buyers like Stan and Sharon want to assume an existing mortgage? Because it's an easy, quick and inexpensive way to find a mortgage. As it is already registered on title, Stan and Sharon can avoid the costs of arranging a new mortgage. If the mortgage interest rate is below the "going" rate, Stan and Sharon will save money here, too. But as the loan already exists, its terms are nonnegotiable.

By law a mortgage is automatically assumable by a purchaser of a property unless a restriction on its being assumed appears right in the mortgage. *Without such a limitation, any purchaser can assume any mortgage without having to obtain the lender's approval and without having to qualify for the loan.* Until the mid-1970s virtually all mortgages were silent on the issue of assumability, which allowed any purchaser to automatically take over an existing mortgage. And this is still the law today. Unless the mortgage specifically says something to the contrary, it's the purchaser and the vendor (but not the lender whose money financed the loan) who decide if a mortgage can be assumed.

The sharp rise in interest rates in the early 1980s saw lenders demanding a say on who assumed their mortgages, especially loans carrying a lower-than-market interest rate. Since then three clear positions have evolved on this issue of "assumability":

1) *Fully assumable*: The normal state of the law. If the mortgage is silent on the point, any purchaser could automatically assume any mortgage, without approval.

2) *Fully nonassumable*: The other extreme. Here the mortgage contains a clause specifically making it fully due and payable if the property is sold. In other words, no buyer can assume this mortgage. This clause reflects a recent trend that treats a mortgage like a personal loan, granted to a specific borrower and no one else. The validity of these clauses has been upheld in a number of reported cases.

3) *Possibly assumable, or due on sale at the lender's option*: Also known as an optional maturity clause. The middle ground. This is the most common type of assumable clause appearing in mortgages today. These due-on-sale clauses give lenders a veto by requiring that purchasers be approved to assume a mortgage.

By giving a lender an option to cancel a loan if the borrower sells the property, the ultimate decision now rests with the lender. Due-on-sale clauses also allow lenders to pass judgment on the creditworthiness of a purchaser who wants to take over a mortgage. If a lender says no, the borrower/seller must pay off the loan when the sale closes. Put another way, *with a due-on-sale clause a mortgage can only be assumed when a property is sold if the purchaser applies to assume it, he or she qualifies for it, and the lender permits the buyer to assume the mortgage.* The last point is very important, since not every lender will allow every buyer to assume every mortgage, even if the borrower otherwise qualifies.

Due-on-sale clauses give lenders a significant advantage if a property is sold before the mortgage matures, an advantage few borrowers fully understand. Lewis and Lili booked a mortgage at 12% that contained a due-on-sale clause, and now want to sell their property in midterm. If rates have risen to 15%, the lender can call in the 12% loan (often also charging a prepayment penalty) and relend the money to earn 15%. This is exactly what happened in the early 1980s, when the interest rates on existing mortgages were significantly lower than current rates.

If interest rates have dropped to 9% when the property is sold, most lenders will allow any purchaser to take over the 12% mortgage. What lender would want to cancel a 12% mortgage when current rates are just 9%? But if the purchaser doesn't want to assume the mortgage, the lender will demand that Lewis and Lili pay a prepayment penalty for cancelling the loan early. With due-on-sale clauses, it's a virtual no-lose situation for lenders.

When investigating these clauses, learn what the penalty will be if the lender calls the loan when the property is sold. It could differ significantly from lender to lender. In some cases the borrower will have to pay the same predetermined penalty that applies to any prepayment of the mortgage money (discussed in Chapter 8). But the penalty charged by other lenders when exercising their option to call the loan is *all the interest* to the date of maturity! What an arbitrary and meaningless approach, resulting in windfall profits to lenders.

What information does a lender want in deciding whether the buyer can assume the mortgage? All the same details as if the buyer were booking a new mortgage, discussed in Chapter 2.

Most people believe when a mortgage is assumed by a purchaser on selling their home, their liability ends and that they are off the hook. Not so, much to their surprise and chagrin, unless they live in Saskatchewan or Alberta. Elsewhere in Canada, reported cases have held the original borrower responsible for payment of the principal and interest at the rate stated in the mortgage despite the sale, until the mortgage is fully paid off and discharged. This applies even if the new owner renews the mortgage! Far and away this continued liability "on the covenant" is one of the major drawbacks with assumable mortgages.

The rule that the assumption of an existing mortgage by a purchaser (Jill) did not release the original borrower (Cheryl) arose at a time when all mortgages were automatically assumable. And the rule made sense then. A mortgage is a contract where the original borrower agrees in writing to repay the borrowed money plus interest. The lender (Easy Money Ltd.) had absolutely no say in deciding whether Jill could take over the mortgage, no opportunity to check Jill's credit rating. Therefore the amount outstanding should be recoverable from either Cheryl or Jill, but not both, if Jill later defaults in paying the mortgage.

Practically speaking, most lenders only proceed against the current owner of the property. Realistically, Cheryl need only worry if land values have fallen so dramatically that the property is worth less (only $90,000) than the amount owing on the mortgage ($100,000). Still, imagine Cheryl's potential shock to learn, possibly years after selling the property, that she might have to pay the $10,000 deficiency between what's owing on the mortgage and the price for which Jill sold the property.

What if purchasers like Jill must be approved to assume an existing mortgage because the mortgage had a due-on-sale clause? In contrast to the automatically assumable mortgage, "assuming with approval" an existing mortgage would closely parallel arranging a new $100,000 mortgage. In both cases Jill would have to file exactly the same information with Easy Money Ltd. *and receive its formal approval* before being allowed to receive the money/assume the mortgage. In both cases a conscious decision would have to be made based on her creditworthiness.

If Jill booked a new mortgage and later fell behind in payments, Easy Money Ltd. would have no right to sue the old borrower, Cheryl. If Jill instead assumed Cheryl's old mortgage *with the lender's express approval* and if Jill later fell behind in payments, why should Easy Money Ltd. still be able to sue Cheryl? Why should a lender be in a better position (being able to sue either the original borrower or the purchaser) if the purchaser gets the lender's express consent to assume an existing mortgage, than if the purchaser is arranging a new mortgage? It shouldn't. But the current state of the law puts lenders in that better position, and that is unfair.

Change is in the wind. The Ontario Law Reform Commission in its 1987 study on mortgages recommended the following for residential mortgages. If enacted, Cheryl's liability as original borrower would automatically end when the property is sold to a purchaser like Jill who is approved by the lender to assume the mortgage. A sound recommendation, as it properly equates new mortgage loans and assumptions with the lender's approval. It will close the gap between reality and the public's perception of reality. As should be the case, the only person on the hook will be the new owner, not the old owner/original borrower.

Until then, what should a borrower like Cheryl do when selling her home if the buyer wants to assume the mortgage? Once a lender gives its consent to a purchaser assuming the mortgage, she should try to get a "release" from the lender. That will relieve Cheryl from any further liability under the mortgage and leave only Jill, the new owner, responsible in case of default. Don't be too optimistic about getting this release. Lenders gain absolutely nothing in giving it, while losing another potential source from whom the mortgage debt can be recovered.

Keep in mind several other points about due-on-sale clauses. Rarely is a due-on-sale clause included in an offer where the seller is to "take back" a mortgage. Therefore, most vendor-take-back mortgages are automatically assumable by subsequent purchasers of the property for this reason.

Before booking a mortgage with a due-on-sale clause, learn if the lender must act "reasonably" in deciding whether to grant its consent. Without this "reasonableness" requirement, lenders can be arbitrary and heavy-handed in preventing a purchaser from assuming the mortgage, despite excellent financial credentials. Or they can be arbitrary and heavy-handed in imposing conditions that must be satisfied before the mortgage can be assumed.

Besides the due-on-sale clause, be on the lookout for its black-sheep cousins, "due on encumbrance" and "due on negotiation" clauses. Avoid them at all costs. With a due-on-encumbrance clause, the lender can cancel Chris's loan if another mortgage is registered on title afterwards. Since it appeared in his first mortgage, this clause effectively prevented Chris from ever obtaining a second mortgage! A due-on-negotiation clause gives the lender the option to cancel the mortgage if the borrower simply starts to negotiate, either for a subsequent mortgage, or to sell the property! Talk about an oppressive clause.

When shopping for the perfect mortgage, try to arrange a loan where the mortgage would be fully assumable on any subsequent sale of the property. If interest rates are high (i.e. 18%), a fully assumable mortgage bearing an interest rate below current rates (say 12%) is a prominent selling feature of a home, just like the finished basement and the new kitchen. If a fully assumable mortgage can't be booked, as a bare minimum insist on a mortgage from category 3—"due on sale at the lender's option." Avoid fully nonassumable clauses at all costs. But remember, not all lenders include due-on-sale clauses in their mortgage packages. As with other features, some do, some don't; it depends on the individual lender.

When Shopping for the Perfect Mortgage, Ask:

1) If the property is sold before the mortgage matures, is it fully assumable? fully nonassumable? due on sale at the lender's option?
2) What will the penalty be if the lender will not allow the buyer to assume the mortgage?
3) If a purchaser is approved to assume an existing mortgage, will the lender give a release to the original borrower?
4) Must the lender act "reasonably" in deciding whether to grant its consent to a buyer assuming the mortgage?
5) Does the mortgage contain "due on encumbrance" and "due on negotiation" clauses?

15
The Portable Mortgage

Take the mortgage with you when you move

What is a portable mortgage? Portable TVs are designed to be taken easily from place to place. And there are portable radios, portable telephones and even portable computers. But a portable mortgage?

Welcome to a new feature offered by some (but not all) mortgage lenders. Just like a TV, the portable mortgage is designed to be easily taken from one place to another. It's a very practical idea, providing flexibility to borrowers with long-term loans who sell one house and buy another before the mortgage matures. With portability, an existing mortgage is removed from title to the old house and reregistered against the new house. Practically speaking, borrowers can shift their current mortgage from one house to another, just like their furniture, and eliminate all prepayment penalties! By safeguarding the interests of homeowners/borrowers who sell their home in midterm, portability is an essential element of the perfect mortgage.

Consider the dilemma Sam and Judy faced when buying a house, unaware of the portability option. Rates for long-term (five-year) loans were quite good (12%), but so were short-term (one-year) rates (10.5%). While they considered a shorter-term mortgage, Sam and Judy really wanted the security of a five-year term. But was a long-term mortgage the right choice for them?

Sam and Judy knew that more than just rate must be considered in selecting a mortgage term, such as their anticipated period of ownership. If they didn't intend to remain there for more than three or four years, they shouldn't select a mortgage term longer than that. But Sam and Judy weren't too sure how long that house would be able to service their needs—maybe three years, maybe five. If they booked a long-term mortgage, maybe they would sell the house before the mortgage came due, maybe not. But here they were, debating the sale of a house they had not even bought yet!

Sam and Judy knew that if they booked a five-year mortgage and sold the house three-and-a-half years later to a purchaser who did not want to assume the mortgage, a large prepayment penalty would have to be paid to cancel it. (The size of the penalty, and whether it could be set arbitrarily by the lender, depended in which Chapter 8 category the prepayment clause fell.)

Yet if they sold this house during the term of the mortgage, Sam and Judy probably would be "trading up," buying a larger and more expensive home, financing it with a larger and more expensive mortgage. What a strange situation that would be— paying a penalty to break one mortgage, and then borrowing back the same money (and maybe more) from the same lender, possibly at a higher rate of interest! Sam and Judy were really unsure what to do.

Then Sam and Judy learned about portability, and immediately realized this was the answer to their dilemma. How portability changed their strategy on booking a mortgage! As a nonnegotiable "need" on their needs and wants list, Sam and Judy shopped and shopped and shopped until they found a lender that included portability right in the mortgage. It was *the* factor behind their choice of both a long-term mortgage and a lender.

How did portability "sell" Sam and Judy on the long-term mortgage? Say they booked a five-year portable mortgage and then sold their house in midterm. The existing mortgage (with the same outstanding balance, interest rate, maturity date and other features) would be "ported" from the old house to the new house, provided the usual income and property value criteria continued to be satisfied. By doing this, the prepayment penalty otherwise payable on the sale of the property would be totally eliminated! All other factors remaining the same, all that changed as a result of the "port" was the security for the loan!

As Sam and Judy learned, portability makes the long-term mortgage viable. Without portability, the borrower must decide where he or she will be when the mortgage matures, even before the mortgage is arranged or renewed! With portability, borrowers no longer have to predict the future. Portability means borrowers do not have to be committed to owning one specific home for the entire mortgage term; they only have to be *committed homeowners* for the entire mortgage term. And that's a big, big difference.

Tony and Anna's situation was slightly different. In hindsight, were they ever glad they included the portability option in their mortgage. They booked the $100,000, 12% mortgage with Angel Trust shown on page 135, having a term of five years. It was a category 3 (limited open—10% prepayment privilege only) mortgage. After four years, when the outstanding balance was $96,591.00 they decided to sell their home and buy another one. The purchaser did not want to assume the mortgage. Only one problem. Tony and Anna needed another $60,000 to finance their new home purchase. Rates for one-year mortgages (the remaining time left on their old mortgage) had fallen 2% to 10%.

One alternative was to pay off the existing mortgage, and then arrange a new mortgage either with the current lender or another lender. When Tony and Anna asked about the prepayment penalty, the lender arbitrarily selected three months' interest, or $2,827.83 (the interest component of the next payment [payment 49] or $942.61 multiplied by three). Quite a large sum. But the new $160,000 one-year mortgage would carry a lower interest rate—10%.

Instead of paying off the existing mortgage at considerable expense, Tony and Anna considered porting the mortgage to the new house. Unfortunately the "ported" mortgage wouldn't provide Tony and Anna with enough money to complete the purchase; they were about $60,000 short. However, besides providing portability, their mortgage also contained a "port/increase/blend" feature, provided the property value and income criteria continued to be met. The so-called "old" money (money ported from the old house) would be blended with the "new" money (additional money being advanced now for the first time) to produce an effective rate of interest that acknowledged the proportion of each. Called a "weighted average" by lenders, it's just like blending together different colours of paint in a hardware store, or mixing different ingredients together in a food processor.

Therefore, what appeared to be a problem was no problem at all. The "old" money, $96,591.00, represented 60.37% of the $160,000 now being borrowed, while the "new" money, the amount of the increase, made up the remaining 39.63%. What would the new, weighted rate be for Tony and Anna's one-year mortgage?

12% times 60.37% =	7.244%
10% times 39.63% =	3.963%
TOTAL	11.207%

rounded up to 11.25%. By combining old money with new money, the new interest rate for Tony and Anna's one-year mortgage would be 11.25%, *and no prepayment penalty at all would have to be paid*.

Tony and Anna were happy. Although they were paying a higher rate on the new mortgage (11.25%) than current rates for an equivalent-term mortgage (10%), their cash flow was not devastated by any prepayment penalty. And their lender was happy. Not only did it keep a customer and a $96,500 loan, it advanced an additional $60,000 to borrowers with a proven track record. The interest rate and the subsequent monthly payment were set blending the old and new components, stirring both parts together to arrive at a figure that was fair to both parties.

When considering a port/increase/blend, be on the lookout for lenders that fail to both blend the rates and eliminate the penalty. Occasionally in a port-and-increase situation, as with Bill and Mary, while the lender charged no prepayment penalty, it did not blend the rate to give them the benefit of the current (lower) rate of interest on the "new" money borrowed. Their lender felt the elimination of the prepayment penalty was a large enough benefit. As it felt that giving Bill and Mary a reduced rate of interest would be a windfall the lender charged the old (higher) rate of interest on the entire amount now borrowed, despite the port and increase. How unfortunate for Bill and Mary that while the lender offered portable mortgages, it did not fully understand the essentials of that product.

In Tony and Anna's situation, the mortgage interest rate was higher than current rates. The reverse was the case in Archie and Edith's situation—the interest rate on their mortgage was lower than current rates. They too booked a $100,000, five-year, 12%, category 3 (limited open—10% prepayment privilege) mortgage, shown on page 135, with their lender, Shyster Trust. Archie and Edith also decided to sell their home and buy another one after four years, when the outstanding balance was

$96,591.00. Archie and Edith also needed another $60,000 more to finance their new home purchase. But here, rates for one-year mortgages (the remaining time left on their old mortgage) had increased by 2% to 14%.

While the purchaser wanted to take over this mortgage, carrying an interest rate 2% below the going rate, Archie and Edith wanted to keep it too. "Porting/increasing/blending" like Tony and Anna did would be ideal for Archie and Edith, as it would ensure that the new, combined rate reflecting old money (at below market rates) and new money (at current interest rates) would be less than the current one-year rate of 14%. The "old" money, $96,591.00, represented 60.37% of the amount now being borrowed, $160,000, while the "new" money (to be lent at 14%) made up the remaining 39.63%. If Archie and Edith could port, increase and blend, the combined rate for their one-year mortgage would be:

12% times 60.37% =	7.244%
14% times 39.63% =	5.548%
TOTAL	12.792%

which was rounded up to $12\frac{7}{8}\%$. *Since they could keep the lower rate on the old money for the remainder of the mortgage term, Archie and Edith would not have to pay current interest rates for the full amount of the mortgage, and no prepayment penalty would have to be paid either.* What a wonderful thought.

Unfortunately Archie and Edith learned the hard way why including portability right in the mortgage is so important. Like most lenders, Shyster Trust did not offer the portability option, and refused to allow them to "port" the mortgage. The result? Archie and Edith had no alternative but a) pay off the existing mortgage with a prepayment penalty and b) arrange a new mortgage at current rates for their new home purchase either with the present lender or another one.

What a travesty for Archie and Edith. Paying a large penalty to cancel the old mortgage was bad enough. (Shyster Trust, exercising its absolute discretion, chose three months' interest or $2,827.83 as the penalty despite the increase in rates, the same as Tony and Anna would have paid when rates had fallen.)

And then they lost the benefit of that 12% mortgage. *And then* Archie and Edith had to book a new mortgage at current rates, 14%, on money previously borrowed at 12%!

Considering the way Shyster Trust treated them, it was understandable why Archie and Edith decided to look elsewhere for a new mortgage. They had only one word for the Shyster lenders—greedy. But it suffered in the long run, too. Not only did it lose a $96,500 loan but, more importantly, a customer, because Archie and Edith transferred all their business away from Shyster Trust: savings account, term deposit, credit card and RRSP. If only Shyster Trust had offered portability. . . .

What are some of the questions to ask about portability when shopping for the perfect mortgage? What information has to be provided to the lender in order to port or port/increase/blend the mortgage? Because it is being registered against the new house, borrowers usually must file a formal application for the mortgage as if it were a new loan, and then satisfy the lender's usual requirements—income and property value qualification.

If the ported amount is being increased (such as Tony and Anna's was), be sure the term for the "new" money (and the rate applied in blending) is the same as the remaining term for the "old" money. In their situation, the remaining term for the old money was one year, although the original term of the mortgage was five years. When the mortgage was ported/increased/blended, the new rate blended with Tony and Anna's old rate was the one-year rate in effect at the time of the blending. Therefore, the maturity date for the new, larger mortgage was exactly the same as the maturity date for the original mortgage—one year from the date of blending. Different maturity dates will make it virtually impossible to properly blend the rates, since the components being mixed together don't properly match.

What fees will apply if you port, or port/increase/blend? Certainly the usual charges will apply. But will the lender levy any "administrative" fee or extra charge if you invoke the portability provision?

As shown in the above examples, rarely is the blended rate an exact figure. What happens then? Is it rounded up to the nearest $\frac{1}{8}$%? The nearest $\frac{1}{4}$%? Make sure the answer is clearly spelled out, right in the mortgage.

Not everyone will need to port, or port/increase/blend. Some borrowers, like Steve and Ruth, will be "trading down," buying a smaller house with a smaller mortgage, while their current mortgage is outstanding. What then?

Steve and Ruth originally booked the $100,000, 12% mortgage shown on page 135, with a term of five years. After four years, when the outstanding balance was $96,591.00, they decided to sell their home and buy another one. As they didn't need such a large mortgage—$75,000 would suffice—they ported just $75,000 of their current mortgage. They paid the appropriate prepayment penalty on the $21,591.00 they didn't need, and were prepaying. Simple enough—provided the mortgage contains a "port and reduce" clause, as theirs did.

Remember that the portability feature must appear right in the mortgage document. Too many Canadian institutional lenders today promote portability in their advertising brochures, but do not include it in their mortgage documents. What does this mean for the borrower? It's not a portable mortgage. That's right, there is no written legal obligation by the lender that allows you to port the mortgage if specified criteria are met. Portability in this situation is nothing more than a "policy" offered by the lender. And as we have seen, policy programs can change overnight, to the detriment of the borrower.

Not everybody takes out a mortgage and then owns the property until full term. By taking the risks (and the penalties) out of the long-term mortgage, the portable option offers solid protection for committed homeowners who decide to sell their home before the mortgage matures. It's another example of how the mortgages of today are personalized loans given to borrowers, tailored to their unique circumstances, but still secured by land. Portability is an essential safeguard to include when shopping for the perfect mortgage. Its availability could be *the* determining factor in choosing a mortgage.

When Shopping for the Perfect Mortgage, Ask:

1) Is the mortgage portable from one place to another?
2) Does the mortgage include just a straight "port," or a "port/increase/blend" feature? What about port and reduce?
3) What information has to be provided to the lender in order to port/increase/blend the mortgage?

4) In the case of a port/increase/blended mortgage, will the term of the new, larger mortgage be the same as the remaining term for the original mortgage?
5) What fees will apply if you port, or port/increase/blend?
6) To what figure is the interest rate rounded?
7) Does the portability feature exist right in the mortgage, or is it just the lender's policy to allow the mortgage to be ported?

16
Renewals/Early
Renewals

How to secure the best rate for a longer term

A common misconception is that lenders must renew mortgages when they mature. Wrong, wrong, wrong. By law, mortgages are not automatically renewable when they come due. In fact, the reverse is true—when the mortgage matures, the borrower technically must repay the loan. There's no obligation for lenders to renew a mortgage, unless a right of renewal specifically appears in the loan document. Since most mortgages are silent on the point, most mortgages are not renewable on maturity.

While Vince's mortgage legally must be repaid when the mortgage comes due, many institutional lenders do have a policy of renewing mortgages on maturity. (Other options are examined in Chapter 20.) Whether an institutional lender will exercise the option in Vince's favour depends on his history as a borrower, the property, the state of the market and the lender's policy on renewals. Always remember that if the mortgage is silent, lenders have an absolute discretion in renewing a mortgage. Discretionary policy is subject to change without notice.

If Vince has been persistently late in making his payments, or if his property has fallen in value impairing the security for the loan, even an institutional lender may be reluctant to renew the loan. If interest rates have increased significantly since the loan was booked, an institutional lender might refuse to renew, if it feels Vince will be unable to handle the higher payment.

Too many borrowers learned this lesson the hard way in the early 1980s, with interest rates upwards of 20%, when institutional lenders would not renew mortgages. However, if the loan is well secured and the borrower is both prepared and able to pay current rates, most institutional lenders will not look elsewhere for a source to place their funds. Still, nothing changes the fact that a mortgage is not automatically renewable unless a "renewal" clause appears right in the mortgage. Because the lender holds all the cards, there is no guarantee Vince will be offered a renewal, or that his request for a renewal will be granted.

Private lenders are different. Unless they are in the business of lending money, most individual lenders will not renew a mortgage with Vince, despite his credit history. This is one of the major drawbacks of arranging mortgages with private lenders.

Since the perfect mortgage would give borrowers like Ian and Marie the automatic right to renew their mortgage if certain specified criteria were satisfied, what are they? Obviously, Ian and Marie must be up-to-date with all obligations under the mortgage. Lenders will only renew a loan if the borrower *is not* in default. Make sure the words "is not" have not been replaced by the expression "never has been." Otherwise, *any* breach by Ian and Marie, any late payment of even one day, even if it has since been corrected, and the right to renew is lost forever.

When will the renewal notice be sent to Ian and Marie? Thirty days before the mortgage matures? Fifteen days? Sixty days? Will it be on the same terms as those granted to new borrowers? Don't scoff; many lenders in the past charged a higher rate of interest to existing borrowers like Ian and Marie, knowing the cost of changing lenders is virtually prohibitive. (This situation is improving, though, as will be seen in Chapter 20.)

What will the cost be for the renewal? Ian and Marie would prefer if the fee appeared right in the mortgage, so they would immediately know the cost. Too often, though, the renewal fee will be "the lender's current charge at the time of the renewal," an amount that is subject to change. What that figure will be is anybody's guess, although it usually is around $100.

Normally the renewal agreement containing the new interest rate is sent to the borrowers during the last 15 to 30 days of the mortgage term. Borrowers whose mortgages are coming up for maturity always fear another round of interest-rate increases just before it actually matures. However, a new mortgage feature, the early renewal option, allows mortgages to be renewed *at any time during the last year of the mortgage term*, instead of only at the end of the mortgage term. Its value to borrowers who are worried that interest rates will be higher when the mortgage matures should not be underestimated. Its inclusion in the perfect mortgage, especially where the borrower is planning to stay in the house on a long-term basis, should not be overlooked.

Jeffrey and Donna booked the $100,000, five-year, 12% mortgage appearing on page 135. Interest rates were quite stable during the first four years, but then went on a roller-coaster ride. At the start of the fifth year, rates for a five-year mortgage were 12%, with nine months left in the term they fell to 11%, with six months to go they returned to 12%, three months before maturity they rose to 13.5%, and fell back to 13% by maturity. Oh, if they could have only renewed their mortgage earlier than the end of the fifth year!

But they did! Because their mortgage contained the early renewal feature, Jeffrey and Donna could decide at any time during the last year of the mortgage term when to renew their mortgage. Unlike most borrowers, they didn't have to agonize about what the interest rate would be until virtually the very last day of term. Were they ever glad they insisted on including "early renewal." Effectively it allowed them to refinance their mortgage when interest rates were at their lowest.

What did early renewal do for Jeffrey and Donna? First, it gave them a right to renew the mortgage, a significant departure from the norm. More importantly, early renewal eliminated the uncertainty about interest rates. Without early renewal, it's virtually luck of the draw where rates might be when the mortgage matures. But not for Jeffrey and Donna. By exercising the early renewal option, they acquired the security of a long-term (five-year) mortgage at nominal cost. The term and rate for the renewal mortgage were those offered by the lender at the time Jeffrey and Donna exercised the early renewal option, not those in effect when the mortgage matured. And renewing early saved Jeffrey and Donna a lot of money, too. Early renewal sounds too good to be true.

How does the idea work? Jeffrey and Donna exercised their early renewal right with nine months left in their five-year, 12% mortgage, after payment 51 was made. The amount outstanding on the loan at that time was $96,320.51. The mortgage would be renewed for a new five-year term, at 11%. To take advantage of early renewal, all they had to do was apply to the lender in writing to renew the mortgage now, not in nine months' time.

Understandably, the lender wanted some sort of compensation for the early renewal. After all, it was allowing a 12% mortgage to be renewed nine months early. What was the penalty Jeffrey and Donna had to pay for the early renewal? $657.07. In other words, by paying $657.07 Jeffrey and Donna renewed their 12% mortgage nine months early for a further term of five years, but now at 11%. They were also able to avoid an interest rate of 13%, the rate they would have paid if they waited until the mortgage actually matured. Wonderful. But how was this strange figure, $657.07, calculated?

The early renewal clause in Jeffrey and Donna's mortgage said the penalty for renewing the mortgage during the last year of the mortgage term would be the present value of the difference in the interest rates (contractual vs. current) on the outstanding principal for the balance of the mortgage term. If this sounds familiar, it is—it's the interest rate differential explained in Chapter 12! As was discussed there, the IRD approach gives lenders their just due, without creating windfall profits.

In Jeffrey and Donna's case, the $96,320.51 outstanding principal was processed through the IRD formula, using the 1% difference in interest rates (12% contractual vs. 11% current) for the nine months remaining in the mortgage term. In raw numbers, the penalty would be $96,320.51 times 1% times nine-twelfths (the number of months left in the mortgage term over the number of months in the year), or $722.40. When the present value of that number was determined (recognizing how the penalty itself would generate interest over those nine months), the result was $657.07.

By adapting the IRD to early renewals, Jeffrey and Donna's lender properly recognized that early renewal really is nothing more than a prepayment of the mortgage. Effectively, Jeffrey and Donna are retiring their 12% mortgage nine months early, and then booking a new mortgage at 11%. Viewed as a prepayment, the penalty would be the IRD. Viewed as an early renewal, the cost would be the IRD. Either way, the amount Jeffrey and Donna would pay to cancel the old arrangement and arrange the new mortgage is the same—the IRD, or $657.07. Adapting the IRD approach to early renewals gives increased credibility to the IRD as the appropriate penalty to charge borrowers prepaying their loans.

As is the case with other features making up the perfect mortgage, not all lenders offer an early renewal feature. Some do, some don't; it depends on the particular lender. Since the early renewal option really is a limited application of the interest rate differential approach, lenders who use the IRD as their prepayment penalty should also offer an early renewal option. If they don't, the lender's sincerity about guaranteeing a mortgage renewal is questionable. After all, these lenders allow borrowers like Ted and Mary to use the IRD to fully pay off their mortgage. But they will not permit Ted and Mary to use the IRD to renew their mortgage before it matures. Why the inconsistency?

But the reverse is even more ironic. Some Canadian lending institutions apply the IRD in offering early renewal, a prepayment during the last year of the mortgage term. But they do not accept the IRD as the basis for *all* prepayments! Why they approve the concept in one limited situation but not another is baffling. Yet this is the current state of the mortgage market with many lenders today. It explains why carefully shopping for a mortgage is so important.

Assuming a lender offers the early renewal option, when can it be exercised? Most institutional lenders only allow it during the last year of the mortgage term. Since the penalty is the interest rate differential, there is no reason why the eligibility period must be limited this way. In fact, if the lender offers the IRD as the prepayment penalty, effectively that should give the borrower the right to renew the mortgage *anytime* he or she wants. After all, the penalty charged for the early renewal, even during the third year of a five-year term, will be the present value of the difference in the interest rates on the outstanding balance for the remainder of the mortgage term. Why restrict its usefulness further?

What if Jeffrey and Donna had exercised the early renewal option six months before their mortgage matured? At that time their mortgage rate was identical to the "going" rate, 12%. Applying the IRD approach—the basis for an early renewal—the difference in the interest rates would have been 0%. This means Jeffrey and Donna could have renewed their mortgage six months before maturity for another five years, at no cost! Of course, the rate of interest for the renewal term here would have been 12%.

This is probably the greatest practical benefit of the early renewal feature—the opportunity to extend the mortgage for a long term, *at no cost,* if the rate of interest during the last year of the mortgage is the same as the rate of interest the borrowers are currently paying. It's a straightforward idea that everyone can understand. Security, stability, peace of mind—all these can be achieved for another five-year period simply by renewing the mortgage at the same rate of interest *during* the last year of the mortgage term, instead of waiting until the mortgage matures.

Why do some lenders offer early renewal today? The mortgage market is very competitive, forcing lenders to work harder than ever to generate new business and retain old commitments. Changing lenders on maturity has never been easier or cheaper for borrowers. Lenders offering early renewal are giving borrowers opportunities that never existed before. With early renewal the borrower has a guaranteed right that the mortgage will be renewed. Borrowers can take advantage of a drop in interest rates, at a cost that is fair to both lenders and borrowers. And they can even extend their mortgage at no cost by exercising the early renewal option when the mortgage rate and current rates are the same. By adopting the early renewal option, some lenders are demonstrating their sincerity in keeping you and your mortgage.

Early renewal turns borrowers into interest-rate watchers during the last year of the mortgage term. It also turns them into modern-day clairvoyants trying to decide when is the best time to exercise the early renewal option. But is this so bad? Most people whose mortgages are maturing will be following interest rates closely anyway. Why not have flexibility and the right to seize a good interest rate during the course of the last year of the mortgage term, instead of having to sit on the sidelines until the time is up?

Remember that while a lender may allow an early renewal, the onus clearly is on the borrower to exercise that right. Once an early renewal option is included in a mortgage, it's up to the borrower to use it. If Jeffrey and Donna had done nothing, their lender would send them a mortgage renewal (if that is its policy) within a month of maturity, like usual.

Volatile interest rates have been a fact of life in Canada in the 1980s. The outlook for interest rates, both short term and long term, is not substantially different. Much can happen to interest rates during the course of a year. Look at 1987, where rates hit a low of 10% in early April, increased steadily to 12.25% until October, and then fell back to 11.5% in the wake of the stock market crash. Borrowers without early renewal options were hamstrung; they could not take advantage of any dips in the rates. But borrowers with early renewal options could renew their commitments for long terms at no, or nominal, cost.

Early renewals are an important component of the perfect mortgage, providing protection against the suspense of the interest-rate saga. Avoid being a borrower who downplays the importance of the early renewal option, and later regrets not having it.

When Shopping for the Perfect Mortgage, Ask:

1) Is the mortgage *automatically* renewable when it matures, or is it renewable only at the lender's option?
2) What criteria and conditions must be satisfied in order to renew the mortgage? Must the borrower be "not in default," or "never in default"?
3) When will notice of the renewal be given? Will it be on the same terms as those granted to new borrowers? What will the cost be? Is it a fixed amount, or just the lender's current charge at the time of the renewal?
4) Does the lender offer "early renewal"? During what period of time—the last year before maturity only? What compensation is the lender seeking for early renewal?

17
The Convertible Mortgage

The "lock-in" privilege

Chapter 15 examined "portable" mortgages—a mortgage that could easily be taken from one home to another. But what is a "convertible" mortgage? When it comes to cars, "convertible" means easily changeable from one form to another form. How does this apply to mortgages?

"Convertible" mortgages, also called the "lock-in privilege," are a variation of the early renewal option discussed in the last chapter. Where the mortgage is convertible, it can easily be changed from one form to another, converted from a short-term to a long-term mortgage. How does it work, why is it necessary, and when is it most beneficial?

Just as portability makes the long-term mortgage viable, convertibility makes the short-term mortgage viable. Eddie and Ellen arranged a short-term (six month) mortgage at 11%. What if interest rates started to rise during that six-month period? Would they have to wait until the six-month term was up before being able to renew the mortgage? Or could they "convert" the loan into a longer-term mortgage, and "lock in" to a good interest rate during the course of that six-month term, just like an early renewal? This second option is what they really wanted. So when shopping for a mortgage, Eddie and Ellen made sure their mortgage was convertible.

The convertible feature provides considerable flexibility to borrowers who arrange short-term mortgages. As will be seen in Chapter 19, one of the prime reasons for a short-term mortgage is the lower interest rates they offer. This benefit could easily be lost if the borrower could not convert the loan to a long-term, fixed-rate mortgage *whenever he or she wanted*, before the short-term mortgage matured. For anyone booking a short-term mortgage, this lock-in privilege should be a nonnegotiable feature, as it gives borrowers the lower costs of a short-term mortgage, plus the potential safeguards (if needed) of a long-term loan.

What safeguards should Eddie and Ellen include when booking a mortgage with a right-to-convert clause? First, how much notice must be given to the lender in order to exercise this feature? When interest rates are on the rise, time is of the essence. Talk about an imminent increase in interest rates usually precedes the actual hike. If Eddie and Ellen must give their lender a month's written notice, that defeats the purpose of being able to lock in quickly at a current rate. Eddie and Ellen should ensure they can convert at any time immediately after giving written notice to the lender.

Are there any limitations on the type of mortgage to which Eddie and Ellen can convert? Must they lock in to a five-year mortgage, or can they select any other term the lender offers? This is important, as some of the other features in the lender's package (or your own circumstances) may make a commitment that long unattractive. It's always best for borrowers like Eddie and Ellen to keep their options open.

How much will it cost Eddie and Ellen to trigger this lock-in privilege? This is an important consideration, as it could be the ultimate factor affecting their decision. Will there be any administrative fee? Usually there is, just as Eddie and Ellen would face an administrative fee on renewing the mortgage. Is it a predetermined amount, appearing right in the mortgage? Or is it a "reasonable" fee that is subject to change, where the amount charged is the lender's usual fee for such conversions at the time it is exercised? While Eddie and Ellen would prefer the first choice, usually the second scenario applies.

What has to be done to complete the conversion process? The more expensive route would see Eddie and Ellen registering a new mortgage with the new terms, and then cancelling or "discharging" the old mortgage. To save money, some (but not all) lenders will have Eddie and Ellen sign a mortgage-amending agreement that may or may not be registered on title. This way the old mortgage continues to exist, properly amended to reflect the new terms.

Is there any penalty payable for the conversion? Just like an early renewal, locking in to a long-term mortgage really is nothing more than a prepayment. What Eddie and Ellen are doing, effectively, is fully paying off their 11% short-term mortgage early, and then arranging a new mortgage. Therefore, when booking the convertibility feature, and later when exercising it, Eddie and Ellen must be concerned about the prepayment privilege appearing in their mortgage.

As will be seen in Chapter 19, short-term mortgages often are fully open. If this was the case, Eddie and Ellen could convert their short-term loan to a long-term mortgage and pay no pre-payment penalty, regardless of the rate being charged on the new mortgage. On the other hand, if their short-term mortgage were fully closed, Eddie and Ellen could not convert to a long-term mortgage without paying whatever penalty their lender exacts in its discretion. A fully closed mortgage effectively de-feats the advantage of a right-to-convert.

Sometimes the mortgage is silent on allowing the borrower to convert the mortgage to a long-term loan, but it does contain the early renewal option. This was exactly Eddie and Ellen's situation. Since early renewal is an effective substitute for a lock-in clause, it underscores the need for borrowers to include the early renewal feature in their mortgage. Unless the mortgage was fully open, the penalty for converting to a long-term mort-gage applying early renewal would be the IRD—the interest rate differential between their mortgage rate (11%) and the current interest rate on the mortgage term they selected.

If five-year rates had fallen to 10%, Eddie and Ellen would have to pay the present value of the difference in interest rates on the amount owing, for the balance of the mortgage term. As their present 11% mortgage would have no more than six months to run, the penalty payable in these circumstances would be small. If five-year rates had increased to 12%, Eddie and Ellen would not have to pay any penalty to lock in to a mortgage of that term. (In fact, as described in Chapter 12, they really should get a rebate if they paid off this loan early, but no lenders are prepared to do this.) And if the rate for a five-year mortgage were 11%, the same rate as Eddie and Ellen were paying for their short-term mortgage, they could convert the loan at no cost, since the interest rate differential would be zero.

What does this mean? While it's preferable to have a con-vertible mortgage that also is fully open, borrowers like Eddie and Ellen should not despair if they have to rely on an early renewal option when locking in to a long-term mortgage. Unless interest rates have fallen substantially since the short-term mort-gage was originally booked, the penalty payable will be slim to none. And even if long-term rates have declined since Eddie and Ellen booked their loan, there is a good chance they will have exercised their right-to-convert long before the long-term rate fell significantly below their short-term rate. Simply put, it is highly unlikely Eddie and Ellen will pay much (if any) prepayment penalty under any circumstances converting their short-term mortgage into a long-term loan.

As always, make sure the convertibility clause appears right in the mortgage. Never rely on policy—it is not the type of legal commitment borrowers can enforce if overturned in the future.

With a convertible mortgage, borrowers with short-term mortgages give themselves the ultimate in flexibility, whether they want to go short term or long term. Convertibility is one of the key ingredients to consider when shopping for, and booking, the perfect mortgage.

When Shopping for the Perfect Mortgage, Ask:

1) Is the mortgage convertible, allowing the borrower to "lock in" to a fixed-rate, long-term mortgage?
2) How much notice must be given to the lender in order to convert the mortgage?
3) Are there any limitations on the type of mortgage to which the existing mortgage can be converted?
4) How much will it cost to exercise this lock-in privilege—an administrative fee? a prepayment penalty?
5) What has to be done to complete the conversion process—a new mortgage or a mortgage-amending agreement?
6) If the mortgage does not contain a lock-in clause, does it contain the early renewal option instead?

18
Second Mortgages vs. Mortgage Payment Insurance

Second mortgages are usually cheaper

As we saw early on, there are only two ways to pay for a house—with your money or someone else's. When the money comes from someone else, it generally is secured by a mortgage.

Conventional mortgages are only available for 75% of a property's appraised value (or, in the language of the lenders, if the loan-to-value ratio is 75% or less). Elliott and Mandy are thinking of buying a house for $200,000. Since their down payment is $30,000, they will need to borrow $170,000 to finance the purchase. Just because Elliott and Mandy don't have a big enough down payment to pay 25% of the purchase price on closing doesn't mean they can't buy a house. Instead Elliott and Mandy a) will have to arrange financing that is different from the norm and b) must be earning enough money to finance this large debt. Strong, healthy incomes can sometimes compensate for a smaller than normal down payment.

High-ratio mortgages, where the borrower has less than 25% equity in the property, are riskier investments for lenders. Purchasers like Elliott and Mandy have two choices in this situation, either:
1) Split the financing, and arrange a conventional mortgage for 75% of the property value and a second mortgage for that part of the loan exceeding 75% of its value. Because of its size, the second mortgage is known as a "small second."
2) Arrange one large mortgage with an institutional lender and place "mortgage payment insurance" on the entire loan. Mortgage payment insurance is available through CMHC (Canada Mortgage and Housing Corporation, a government agency) or MICC (the Mortgage Insurance Company of Canada, a private insurer). While institutional lenders

cannot grant a conventional mortgage for more than 75% of the appraised value, they can grant high-ratio loans, if insured. Although the loan is high-ratio, the rate of interest would be the same as for a conventional first mortgage. Don't confuse this type of insurance with life insurance offered by some lenders, that pays off the mortgage if the borrower dies during the mortgage term.

Deciding which option to choose is often difficult for purchasers/borrowers. Emotion often enters the picture, clouding the objectivity that is needed. Many people also have a phobia about second mortgages, feeling they should be avoided at all costs. A second mortgage, Elliott and Mandy were told, is the first step on the road to financial disaster.

When it comes to mortgages, there's too much emphasis on the number of mortgages registered. But that alone doesn't determine the extent of risk or the degree of stability. Some second mortgages are as safe as first mortgages, if the combined total of the two mortgages is less than 75% of the appraised value of the property. Meanwhile, some first mortgages are riskier than second mortgages if the first mortgage exceeds 75% of a property's appraised value.

Instead of the number of mortgages, Elliott and Mandy should be concerned about the amount of money borrowed and their equity position behind it. Two totem poles, each worth $200,000, will explain this. On the first totem pole is one mortgage worth $170,000, running from the top down. At the bottom is Elliott and Mandy, with their $30,000 equity. On the second totem pole are two mortgages—one for $150,000 running from the top down, and one for $20,000 below that. Once again Elliott and Mandy are at the bottom, with $30,000 equity. In both situations their equity in the property is the same, and it's located at the bottom, the top $170,000 being mortgaged. From Elliott and Mandy's point of view, is there any difference between the two totem poles? Everything else being equal, the totem pole selected should best suit their unique circumstances.

Whether they follow the first/second mortgage or the insured mortgage route, extra costs will be incurred. They differ considerably between the two alternatives. With CMHC/MICC mortgage payment insurance, a one-time premium is paid by the borrower *on the entire amount of the mortgage* and not just on the portion exceeding 75% of the appraised value, the high-ratio portion that is at risk. This type of insurance does not come cheap. Insurance premiums currently are 1.25% of the total amount of the mortgage when the loan-to-value ratio is between 75% and 80%, 2% of the total amount of the mortgage when the ratio is 80.1% to 85%, and 2.5% of the total mortgage when the loan-to-value is between 85.1% and 90%. While there is no maximum amount that will be lent, the size of the mortgage is restricted—it cannot exceed 90% of the first $125,000 of appraised value, and 80% of the balance. For a $200,000 house, the maximum insured mortgage would be 90% of $125,000 ($112,500) and 80% of $75,000 ($60,000) or $172,500. The purchaser/borrower must have at least a 10% down payment from his or her own resources. In addition, a processing fee is charged, currently ranging from $75 to $235.

CMHC insurance may also be necessary for certain types of low-ratio loans, for example where a house is insulated with urea-formaldehyde foam insulation. A lower insurance premium is charged when the loan-to-value ratio is less than 75%.

Mortgage insurers require that the entire insurance premium be paid up front, when the mortgage is booked. In Elliott and Mandy's case, since they are borrowing $170,000 on a property worth $200,000, the insurance premium would be $3,400. Unfortunately they do not have an extra $3,400 for closing. If they did, they would be borrowing $3,400 less!

As few, if any, borrowers have this money available on closing, CMHC and MICC allow the $3,400 insurance premium to be added onto the mortgage principal. Result: Elliott and Mandy's mortgage would be registered for $173,400. They would receive $170,000 for closing, while the $3,400 would be paid to the insurer. But now Elliott and Mandy would owe their lender $173,400, or $3,400 more than what they actually borrowed! And they would be paying interest on this $3,400 each month until the mortgage is fully retired, perhaps 25 years from now! Assuming an interest rate of 12%, this insurance premium would cost a further $35.08 a month, and $7,125.38 in interest over the amortized life of the loan.

Payment insurance eliminates the risk to the lender by guaranteeing that the payments would be made, either by Elliott and Mandy, or by the insurer. If Elliott and Mandy default on the mortgage for any reason, perhaps due to a layoff, unemployment or disability, the payment insurance would *not* make the payment for them, thus ending their obligation to make the payment. Instead, CMHC or MICC pays the money to the lender, after which the insurer would pursue Elliott and Mandy for that money. Therefore, while mortgage payment insurance is paid by the borrower, *it protects the lender* by assuring that the loan will be repaid if the borrower defaults.

The other alternative open to Elliott and Mandy is to arrange a conventional first mortgage for 75% of the property value, and a second mortgage for the excess needed. Often a mortgage broker is involved who charges a fee for arranging the second mortgage. Then their lawyer must do extra work on the second mortgage, for which he or she charges a fee. Finally, a higher rate of interest will have to be paid on the second mortgage than on the first mortgage. The actual rate depends on their equity in the property, their strength as borrowers, and the lender. But the need for mortgage payment insurance is eliminated this way.

Which choice is cheaper in the long run—the first/second mortgage or the CMHC-insured loan? The answer is surprising. Elliott and Mandy analyzed the alternatives this way. Recall that their purchase price was $200,000. If they booked one high-ratio $170,000 insured mortgage, the interest rate would be 12%. The insurance premium (2% of the amount borrowed) would be $3,400. The quoted administrative fee would be $75.

On the other hand, if they booked a conventional $150,000 first mortgage, the interest rate would be 12%. The $20,000 small second would carry an interest rate 3% higher, or 15%. Considering their 15% equity in the property, "the first mortgage rate plus 3%" was reasonable and fair. The mortgage broker's fee of $325 was standard in the circumstances, while their lawyer's $250 charge for fees and disbursements also was normal. The additional costs of registering a second mortgage would be $325 plus $250 less the $75 that CMHC would be charging as its administrative fee. Total: $500.

Elliott and Mandy considered the first/second mortgage route first. Although they lacked a good down payment, Elliott and Mandy would put their good incomes to work after closing the purchase. They would watch their expenses carefully, save and save and save, and prepay $6,000 towards the second mortgage each year on the anniversary date. They planned to fully retire the second mortgage in three years this way.

Paying off the second mortgage as quickly as possible is one of the key commitments borrowers must make and uphold if they go the second-mortgage route. Keeping that second mortgage outstanding forever makes no sense; the interest cost will soon destroy any benefits that might arise. Three years to retire the second mortgage is the target set by many people, such as Elliott and Mandy, as it is the longest term usually available for a second mortgage. Once it was paid off three years down the road, Elliott and Mandy would then have just one conventional mortgage.

How would Elliott and Mandy structure their first/second mortgage plan? On the closing date of June 1, 1989, they would book a $150,000, conventional first mortgage at 12%, with a five-year term. Amortized over 25 years, the monthly payment would be $1,547.85. Also to be booked that same day would be a $20,500, 15%, second mortgage with a term of three years. (The additional $500 was the net amount of the brokerage and legal fees they would be paying for the second mortgage.) Amortized over 25 years, the monthly payment on the second mortgage would be $255.46. Their total monthly mortgage expense: $1,803.31.

On June 1, 1990 and again on June 1, 1991, Elliott and Mandy would prepay the sum of $6,000 towards the second mortgage. When it matured on June 1, 1992, the balance owing ($5,245.66) would be paid as well. Over the life of this second mortgage the total interest payable would be $5,942.22.

After this three-year period, the amount owing on the first mortgage would be $146,396.20. Elliott and Mandy would then increase their monthly first mortgage payment by the amount that had previously been paid monthly on the second mortgage. Their aim: to pay the same amount monthly after retiring the second mortgage as before. Starting with July 1, 1992, the new amount being paid monthly on the first mortgage would be $1,803.31.

Structured this way, the total time needed to fully retire the first mortgage would be 16.48 years, and the total interest payable on the first mortgage would be $197,506.14. (This assumes no further prepayments were made.) When this amount is added to the interest payable for the second mortgage, $5,942.22, the total interest payable for both mortgages would be $203,448.36. These figures are the yardsticks against which the one high-ratio mortgage must be compared.

To be consistent, Elliott and Mandy decided to pay *exactly* the same amount of money towards the one high-ratio mortgage, and at the same time, as under the first/second mortgage plan.

With a high-ratio first mortgage, the amount being borrowed June 1, 1989, would be $173,400 ($170,000 principal plus $3,400 insurance premium), a figure that is $2,900 higher than under the first/second mortgage scheme. The monthly payment would be $1,803.31, as with the first/second mortgage arrangement. On June 1, 1990, and again on June 1, 1991, Elliott and Mandy would prepay the sum of $6,000 towards the mortgage, as with the first/second mortgage. Finally, on June 1, 1992, they would prepay $5,245.66, identical to the first/second mortgage plan.

What were the results? With one high-ratio mortgage, the total interest cost to Elliott and Mandy would be $213,961.92, compared to $203,448.46 with a first/second mortgage. The total time needed to retire the one high-ratio mortgage would be 17.10 years (compared to 16.48 if a first/second mortgage were used). And the most interesting figure of all: the amount owing after three years, when the second mortgage was retired (assuming the same prepayments were made on both mortgages) was $149,012.72 for the one high-ratio mortgage vs. $146,396.20 for the first/second mortgage. In other words, despite the additional costs for the first/second mortgage and its higher interest rate, it was still the cheaper route. The $2,900 extra principal on the one high-ratio mortgage had barely been affected by three years worth of payments.

This example explains why high-ratio mortgages are more expensive—the insurance premium is added on to the outstanding principal. Elliott and Mandy thus learned what more and more Canadians have discovered in recent years—that it is cheaper to borrow money by way of a conventional first mortgage and a small second mortgage, than to borrow the same amount of money with one insured high-ratio mortgage *provided* the second mortgage is retired as quickly as possible, within no more than three to four years.

In recent years an increasing number of Canadians have been using the second mortgage vehicle instead of a CMHC/MICC-insured loan when they have less than 25% equity in the property. What impact has it had? In May 1987, Canada Mortgage and Housing Corporation actually *reduced* the insurance premium for loans between 75% and 80% of loan value, from 1.5% to 1.25%, to make mortgage insurance more affordable. When has government in the past cut its fees? Obviously even the government began to realize how first/second mortgages were cheaper for borrowers in the long run.

CMHC also began to offer second-mortgage payment insurance at that time. Recognizing their popularity, CMHC agreed to insure second mortgages carrying first-mortgage interest rates arranged with major institutional lenders, where high-ratio first mortgages normally would be insured, if certain conditions were satisfied. It was a direct response to the claim that insurance premiums were being charged on the entire mortgage loan, when only the part exceeding 75% of the property's appraised value was at risk.

Where only one high-ratio mortgage is arranged, the insurance premiums discussed earlier still apply. However, where a CMHC-insured second mortgage is booked, the insurance premium on that loan will be the lesser of the "usual" CMHC insurance premium on the combined first and second mortgage, and 5% of the amount borrowed on the second mortgage, the minimum-size insurable second mortgage being $10,000. In Elliott and Mandy's case, if they booked a high-ratio first mortgage, the insurance premium would be 2% of $170,000 or $3,400. If they booked an insured second mortgage, the insurance premium would be the lesser of that same $3,400 and $1,000 (5% of the second mortgage amount, which is $20,000). This $1,000 could be added to the outstanding principal the same way as for a high-ratio loan.

Unfortunately for most borrowers, before a CMHC-insured second mortgage will be granted an important qualifier must be satisfied that undermines its effectiveness. Elliott and Mandy cannot get a CMHC-insured second mortgage *unless they assume an existing first mortgage* that has been outstanding for at least one year, and that has been repaid promptly. That first mortgage must be with a lender that is NHA (National Housing Act) approved (such as the major lending institutions), although the first mortgage itself need not have been insured with CMHC. Effectively this means Elliott and Mandy cannot arrange a conventional first mortgage on closing their purchase, and then book a CMHC-insured second mortgage for the shortfall. To have a conventional first mortgage, they must look elsewhere for the small second mortgage. To have a CMHC-insured second mortgage, they must assume an existing first mortgage. They can't have it both ways.

Assuming they qualified for a CMHC-insured second mortgage,

Elliott and Mandy now must compare the cost of the $20,500 second mortgage loan at 15%, against the $21,000 insured second mortgage loan at 12%. To be consistent, in both cases the monthly payment would be the same—$255.46. With a broker-arranged second mortgage, the interest payable on Elliott and Mandy's loan after three years would be $5,942.22 and the amount outstanding on the loan at the end of three years would be $5,245.66. Using a CMHC-insured second mortgage, the interest payable over those three years would be $4,713.23 and the balance owing at the end of the three-year term would be $4,516.66.

As Elliott and Mandy learned, while the first/second mortgage plan would be cheaper than one CMHC-insured high-ratio mortgage, the cheapest arrangement of all might be to arrange a CMHC-insured second mortgage—if they can satisfy the mandatory mortgage conditions and in particular, the need to assume an existing first mortgage. Whether this is true for all borrowers depends on many different factors—the length of time the loans will be outstanding, the interest rates, the brokers/ lawyers fees, the monthly payment, and how much is prepaid each year.

When arranging a second mortgage, remember that either the second mortgage should mature at the same time as the first mortgage, or the second mortgage should contain a "postponement" clause that permits the first mortgage to be renewed or replaced without any difficulty. Without this, the second lender could severely restrict the borrower from changing lenders until the second mortgage matured. The importance of a postponement clause should not be overlooked.

At first glance it would appear that one high-ratio mortgage at the lower, first-mortgage interest rate would be cheaper for borrowers than a first and second mortgage. As Elliott and Mandy (and you) now know, appearances can be deceiving. Do as they did. Analyze the cost of one high-ratio mortgage with an insurance premium against the cost of a conventional first mortgage and a second mortgage (both where the second mortgage comes from a mortgage broker and is CMHC-insured).

In many cases borrowers will want to avoid arranging high-ratio mortgage payment insurance unless absolutely necessary because of its higher cost. On the other hand, the viability of the first/second mortgage plan is a surprise—a pleasant surprise to most people. If there is a "right" answer, it is the alternative that will save you, in your unique circumstances, the most money. The final numbers will determine which route to take.

When Shopping for the Perfect Mortgage:

If borrowing more than 75% of the property value, be sure to compare thoroughly the cost of the first/second mortgage against the CMHC-insured mortgage. Opt for the cheaper alternative.

19
Do You Go for a Short-term or Long-term Mortgage?

The right answer means having the right safeguards

Choosing between a short-term mortgage (six months or a year), a long-term mortgage (five years or more) or something in between is one of the most complex questions borrowers face. It makes them soothsayers when even economists can't agree where interest rates are heading. Furthermore, there is no "right" or "wrong" answer when it comes to selecting a mortgage term— at least not at the outset. Only time will tell if the borrower "gambled and won" or "gambled and lost." That doesn't make the task any easier.

What are the advantages of short-term mortgages? Probably the greatest reason for their popularity is the low interest rate. During periods of interest-rate stability, short-term mortgages are a powerful way to save money. Properly structured, they also allow borrowers to lock in to a long-term commitment if rates start to rise. But short-term mortgages are a ticking time bomb during periods of interest-rate volatility. And if interest rates rise substantially, the average rate for a series of short-term mortgages could be higher than for one long-term mortgage.

On a short-term mortgage, time is of the essence. Borrowers here must constantly monitor the market, and respond quickly to a shift in interest rates. But how does anybody know for certain when rates have bottomed out or peaked? Short-term mortgages are a form of legalized gambling, played by thousands of Canadians.

Why do some people select long-term mortgages? For the stability they provide. With a long-term mortgage, borrowers can close their eyes to interest-rate gyrations for the next three to five years. But they also pay a premium for this security. And if the mortgage lacks the appropriate clauses, retiring it before maturity could mean a sizable prepayment penalty.

For many years, long-term mortgages were the only game in town; there were no short-term mortgages to compete against. Since they were automatically assumable, most purchasers would take over an existing mortgage on closing, popularizing the expression "cash to the mortgage." (If a house was sold for $100,000 and the existing mortgage was $70,000, the amount of money paid by the buyer on closing was $30,000—"cash to the mortgage.")

But the marketplace changed. Long-term mortgages had to compete with the attractiveness of the short-term rate. Other factors downgraded the allure of the long-term mortgage—due-on-sale clauses and substantial prepayment penalties if the mortgage was not assumed on a sale. Today long-term mortgages are making a comeback, offering features unheard of just several years ago. But not all lenders offer these new options for long-term mortgages, making the dilemma even tougher for borrowers.

As discussed in Chapter 4, mortgage terms are closely related to interest rates. Shorter terms generally are cheaper than long-term mortgages. Other issues affecting the decision "whether to go short term or long term" include the spread between short-term and long-term rates, the character and personality of the borrower (are you a risk-taker, prepared to face the interest-rate market every six months or a year), the borrower's unique circumstances such as the expected period of ownership, where interest rates have been in the recent past, and appear to be heading in the foreseeable future.

Deciding whether to go short term or long term is only half the story. Regardless of the route followed, the "right" answer means building several safeguards into the mortgage package booked. These protections, consisting of the perfect mortgage features, will provide borrowers like Al and Toni with the maximum flexibility possible over the term of the mortgage. These safeguards are so important that Al and Toni should consider them to be nonnegotiable when shopping for a mortgage. Without them, Al and Toni could find themselves subject to the whim and discretion of an uncooperative lender.

What should the ideal short-term mortgage do? It would let Al and Toni take advantage of a lower interest rate while still providing them the security of a long-term mortgage if and when they decide to go that route. Since interest rates can go in one of three directions—up, down or stay the same—Al and Toni need protection in all three situations.

To take advantage of a drop in interest rates, Al and Toni would want a short-term, fully open mortgage, discussed in Chapter 8. Anything else is not good enough. If rates fell, it could be prepaid in full at any time without any notice or penalty and a new mortgage could be arranged, either with the current lender or with a new one. (Switching lenders is relatively easy— see Chapter 20.) Without a fully open mortgage, Al and Toni could not pay off the short-term loan until it matured, a restriction that could prevent them from benefiting from a drop in rates.

A convertible mortgage (Chapter 17) would protect Al and Toni if rates were to rise. This lock-in privilege would allow them to convert from a short-term to a long-term fixed-rate mortgage at any time and at nominal cost if interest rates began to escalate. If their mortgage lacked convertibility, Al and Toni would find their hands tied until the mortgage expired. Interest rates could have gone up considerably during that time.

What if interest rates stayed stable during the term of their short-term mortgage? Quite possibly Al and Toni would take another short-term mortgage, especially if it appeared that interest rates might bottom out after the initial mortgage term expired. Therefore Al and Toni should ensure their mortgage is automatically renewable at nominal cost on its maturity, discussed in Chapter 16. This is an important factor, since not all short-term mortgages have a guaranteed renewal.

Just because the short-term rate is lower does not mean Al and Toni should turn their back on the long-term mortgage. If they decided to convert to a long-term mortgage, would they be able to handle the higher rate and payment? This question must be answered now, before booking the short-term mortgage, and not later when the actual conversion to a long-term loan takes place. Therefore, when prequalifying for a mortgage (and later being formally preapproved), Al and Toni did not use the short-term rate of 10.5%. In all their calculations they applied the long-term rate of 12%. Though they would be taking advantage of the attractive short-term rate now, Al and Toni knew they could handle the payments if and when they went long term.

When booking a short-term mortgage, an interesting way to

save money is to make the same monthly payment as if a long-term mortgage (at a higher interest rate) were being booked. Al and Toni did this—and were astounded at the results. When they booked their $100,000 mortgage, interest rates were 10.5% for one-year terms and 12% for five years. The monthly payment for a one-year mortgage would be $928.33, and $1,031.90 for the five-year loan.

Instead of paying $928.33 (the one-year payment) for the one-year loan, Al and Toni decided to pay $1,031.90 (the five-year payment) for the one-year loan. After all, if they had booked a five-year mortgage, they would have had to pay the higher amount. So why not pay the higher amount anyway, even though the term is shorter and the rate is lower? The extra $103.57 monthly would be a prepayment of principal that would save them interest.

By doing this and nothing more, at the end of one year Al and Toni owed $97,792.55 instead of $99,095.66, meaning they paid an extra $1,303.11 off the principal! They also saved $13,036.38 in interest. Not bad for doing virtually nothing!

Now assume Al and Toni booked a long-term loan. Ideally, what should it do? It would recognize that Al and Toni are committed homeowners, but that they are not necessarily committed to owning one particular property for the term of the mortgage. What safeguards should they consider? First of all, there are two distinct possibilities—Al and Toni might sell their house during the five-year term, or they might not. If they didn't sell the house before maturity, Al and Toni probably would need to renew the mortgage. Making the mortgage "automatically renewable" would provide that. But an early renewal feature would ensure that, and more. With early renewal, if Al and Toni decided not to sell their home, they could renew the mortgage at any time during the last year, rather than having to wait until the end of the last year (see Chapter 16).

On the other hand, if Al and Toni sold their home to Karen before the mortgage matured, there are three possible scenarios—Al and Toni want the mortgage ("take it"), Karen wants the mortgage ("leave it"), or no one wants it ("dump it"). (A fourth scenario, where the seller and the buyer both want the mortgage is not allowed. Only one party can have it.)

If Al and Toni want the new mortgage, they would like to be able to take it to their new home. If they need more money to finance the purchase, they would like to "port/increase/blend" the loan. The solution: to include portability in their mortgage, examined in Chapter 15. Portability makes the long-term mortgage viable for those borrowers who change houses before the mortgage matures. Without portability, Al and Toni might face the absurd situation of paying a prepayment penalty for cancelling the mortgage and then borrowing back the same money (possibly more) to finance their new home purchase.

When buying their house, say Karen wants Al and Toni to leave the existing mortgage so she can assume it. Can she? If the mortgage is automatically assumable she can, no questions asked. If the mortgage has a "due on sale at the lender's option" clause she can, if the lender allows her to assume the mortgage. These topics are reviewed in Chapter 14. While automatically assumable is better, there is still a good chance Karen could take over the mortgage even with that type of due-on-sale clause.

If Al and Toni sold their home during the term of the mortgage and no one wanted the mortgage (Karen the purchaser did not want to assume it and they did not want to port it to a new house), they would have to "dump" or cancel it. This begs the question: how "open" is the mortgage? Too often the emphasis on liberal prepayment privileges when booking a mortgage is not fully understood until they have to be used. Then and only then will Al and Toni appreciate the importance of what they have—or have not—done. A fully open mortgage (category 1) could be paid off at any time without charge. Any other category of mortgage would result in some type of prepayment penalty. The amount of the penalty—and whether it is fixed or discretionary—depends on which prepayment category (Chapter 8) applies to the mortgage. More and more this is the scenario today—purchasers arranging their own financing, leaving sellers like Al and Toni to pay off the existing mortgage plus a potentially sizable prepayment penalty.

There is no easy answer to the short-term/long-term dilemma. What borrowers must do is analyze the market, their own individual circumstances *and build the appropriate safeguards into the mortgage document when booking the loan.* This way, whether you select a short-term or long-term mortgage, and no matter where interest rates go, you have a formidable defence against the vagaries of the market and a change of circumstance.

When Shopping for the Perfect Mortgage—Short Term—Ask:

1) Is it fully open, in case rates fall?
2) Is it convertible, if rates rise?
3) Is it automatically renewable, if rates stay stable?

When Shopping for the Perfect Mortgage—Long Term—Ask:

1) If I do not sell my house before the mortgage matures, is the mortgage automatically renewable? Does it also contain an early renewal option?
2) If I sell my house before the mortgage matures:
    i) is it portable if I want the mortgage?
    ii) is it automatically assumable if the buyer wants the mortgage?
    iii) is it fully open (or 100% open with a predetermined penalty) if no one wants the mortgage?

20
What Do You Do When the Mortgage Comes Due?

There's more today than just the three "Rs"

Every mortgage—whether long term or short term; a first or second mortgage; payable weekly or monthly; assumable, renewable, convertible, portable; and despite its prepayment provisions—will mature. What do you do when the mortgage comes due? With more and more borrowers booking short-term mortgages, the question is being asked more frequently than ever.

Until recently, the avenues open to borrowers whose mortgages matured were quite standard. Traditionally the three alternatives—the three "Rs"—were: a) retire the loan; b) renew it with the same lender; and c) refinance the mortgage with a different lender. But that's not the case today. Just as change has affected other areas of mortgage financing, a wider range of options is now available when a mortgage is due. In fact, maturity is an excellent opportunity for existing borrowers to take advantage of some of the new developments at nominal cost, and reduce the extremely high interest cost associated with mortgages.

THE FIRST "R"—RETIRING THE MORTGAGE
This is simple. Just pay the lender what is owing, plus a nominal administrative charge (called a "discharge fee") of $100 to $150 and the mortgage is cancelled. No prepayment penalty has to be paid when retiring the loan at this stage since every mortgage, even the most closed type, is fully open on maturity. In fact, technically the mortgage *must* be paid back in full when it comes due, unless alternative arrangements are made.

THE SECOND "R"—RENEWING THE MORTGAGE

Renewing the mortgage at current interest rates is one of those alternatives. "Staying where you are" always has been the most popular choice for borrowers unable to fully pay off the mortgage on maturity, because it is simple and inexpensive to arrange. Both the cost of refinancing the loan plus the similarity of mortgage product in the marketplace encouraged borrowers to stay put. For a fee (usually between $50 and $150), the lender would prepare a mortgage renewal, setting out all the details of the extended loan—the outstanding principal, the new interest rate, the size of the new payments as well as the term of the mortgage renewal—while reaffirming all other terms.

A variation of renewing the mortgage involves reducing the amount owing and then renewing the loan. Catherine owes $123,456 on her mortgage and wants to renew it for only $100,000. On maturity she would pay $23,456 to her lender, and then renew the $100,000 balance. No penalty is payable when reducing the principal on maturity, since every mortgage is fully open at that time.

When renewing a mortgage, be sure the amortization for the new term is reduced by the number of years the mortgage has already been outstanding to reflect the amortization *remaining* on the old loan. Therefore on maturity of Harvey's mortgage which originally had a two-year term/25-year amortization, the AM for the renewal should not exceed 23 years. Any prepayments should also be taken into account in setting the new amortization. Going back to a 25-year amortization on a renewal or refinancing means Harvey will always be behind the eight ball, unable to ever pay off his mortgage.

Because the cost of refinancing has been so high, some lenders have treated existing mortgage customers more harshly on renewal than potential new customers. While current borrowers might be given interest rate commitments that are good for 30 days, new borrowers would be given a guaranteed interest rate for 60 days! Why? Some lenders would even charge current borrowers on a renewal a higher rate of interest—$\frac{1}{4}$% higher or more—than new clients. Why? Despite these negatives, most borrowers still felt it would be cheaper and easier to stay with the old lender than move elsewhere.

THE THIRD "R"—REFINANCING THE MORTGAGE

For years the primary source of new mortgage business was the home buyer. Yet there were many existing homeowners like Eric, with mortgages coming up for renewal, who were dissatisfied with the narrow package of features offered by their current lender, Byebye Bank. After shopping the market carefully, Eric felt that Welcome Trust would provide him with the greatest number of the perfect mortgage options. While he very much wanted to switch lenders, practically speaking that was not viable. Changing lenders meant refinancing the mortgage, which in turn meant arranging a new loan. As Eric learned, this was an expensive proposition, usually to the point of being prohibitive. Effectively Eric had no choice but to remain where he was.

Unlike a renewal, where the lender did all the work, refinancing the mortgage meant involving a lawyer. Eric would have to register a new mortgage with Welcome Trust, and then discharge or "de-register" the existing mortgage with Byebye Bank. All the charges associated with a home purchase would have to be paid (legal fees, disbursements for a full title search and municipal clearances, appraisal and application fee, sometimes the cost of a new survey). And there would also be one additional charge on a refinancing—the old lender's (Byebye Bank) discharge fee, its charge for preparing, processing and signing the mortgage discharge, usually in the $100 to $150 range.

When the dust settled, only one mortgage would be registered against the title to Eric's property—the new mortgage to Welcome Trust. However, the cost of changing lenders—borrowing from a new lender to retire the same sum owing to another lender—often approached $1,000! No wonder few borrowers refinanced their mortgages on maturity.

THE NEW ALTERNATIVE—"SWITCH OR TRANSFER-IN"

In recent years, the shift to short-term mortgages has been accompanied by the ease in changing lenders. Major institutional lenders in most parts of Canada now offer borrowers like Eric a fourth alternative when their mortgages mature. Called "switch" or "transfer-in," this short-circuited refinancing allows Eric to shift his existing loan from one lender to another lender on maturity easily, quickly, and cheaply. This means Eric can acquire all those perfect mortgage features Welcome Trust is offering and which he finds appealing, without facing a refinancing. No longer must Eric feel locked in to his existing lender, Byebye

Bank. As switching lenders is so easy and inexpensive, fewer and fewer lenders now charge current borrowers a higher rate of interest on maturity than prospective customers. The Canadian borrower has been the big winner from the introduction of "the switch."

While the end result is the same as a refinancing, where Welcome Trust's money is used to satisfy the debt owing to Byebye Bank, the process of getting there is greatly different. Unlike the register/de-register process of a refinancing, on a transfer-in no new mortgage is prepared or registered. Instead, the existing loan is simply transferred by Byebye Bank to Welcome Trust.

This transfer of mortgage (also called an assignment) is registered against Eric's title to give Welcome Trust good title to the old mortgage. To incorporate all the terms and options that will apply between Eric and Welcome Trust (the perfect mortgage features Eric so anxiously sought), a mortgage-amending agreement is then prepared and signed. In it are the exact same clauses that a new mortgage with Welcome Trust would contain. Sometimes this mortgage-amending agreement is registered on title; more often than not it isn't.

All this paperwork is handled by Welcome Trust internally. Since the existing mortgage is transferred rather than cancelled and replaced by a new mortgage, the need for a lawyer can be sidestepped. After all, good title to the transferred mortgage was established several years ago when it was first registered. By eliminating the most expensive component—the lawyer—the switch or transfer-in achieves the net result of a refinancing at a considerably lower cost. In fact, depending on the lender and any "specials" it may be promoting, the cost of changing lenders on maturity may be nominal, or nothing at all!

In order for Eric to switch lenders, what does he have to do? First he will have to formally apply at Welcome Trust for the mortgage, providing the information specified in Chapter 2. In addition he should take along the following papers regarding his house and current mortgage: his deed, a copy of the mortgage being transferred plus any amendments or renewals in effect, the most recent information available about the amount outstanding, a copy of the survey for the property, a copy of the tax bill and a copy of the insurance coverage for the property.

Also, Eric should not wait until just before his mortgage matures before starting the switch process. As this technically is a new loan to Welcome Trust, and it will only "hold the rates" for 60 days, Eric should get the wheels in motion no later than two months before his Byebye Bank mortgage matures. Therefore Eric should be shopping for a mortgage, comparing features and options, at least three months before the mortgage comes due. This gives him enough time to explore, apply, get approved and complete the switch when the old mortgage runs out.

Many ads proclaim that borrowers like Eric can switch lenders on maturity as cheaply as if he renewed with his existing lender. Not so. Despite its attractiveness, the real cost of a transfer-in is somewhat blurred amidst the marketing hype. In reality, the true cost of Eric switching his mortgage to another lender will be more than the $50 to $150 cost of renewing with the existing lender, but just slightly more.

Welcome Trust, the new lender, can control its administrative charges for both the transfer-in as well as the mortgage-amending agreement. It can reduce or even eliminate the $100 fee it charges borrowers who switch their mortgages. This explains the "no-cost" transfer-in sales occasionally offered by some lenders.

However, Welcome Trust has no control over the "transfer-out" fee the old lender, Byebye Bank, will charge Eric. Yes, while the new lender charges a "transfer-in" fee, the old lender will also collect a "transfer-out" fee, a cost too often overlooked. That is why the bold statement, "Switch your mortgage at no charge," is usually qualified by an asterisk saying "existing lender may levy a fee." Lenders that promote a no-charge switch are really telling the public only half the truth. How much is this transfer-out charge? Does it destroy the advantage of switching?

If Eric refinanced his existing mortgage, he would have to pay the old lender, Byebye Bank, a discharge fee generally in the range of $100 to $150 for cancelling the old mortgage. If that same mortgage were switched instead from Byebye Bank to Welcome Trust, the old lender is entitled to a fee for preparing, processing and signing the transfer of mortgage. Either way—refinancing or switching—a document is needed from Byebye Bank confirming that no further money is owning to it. From the old lender's perspective, it makes no difference if that document is a cancellation of the loan (for a discharge), or a transfer of the loan to another lender (on a transfer-in). The transfer-out charge, therefore, should approximate the old lender's discharge fee—$100 to $150. Any significantly higher figure is unjustified, considering the similarity of the two documents and the complexity of preparing both.

Combined, the transfer-out and transfer-in fees would be $100 to $150, plus $100, for a total of $200 to $250 (although the second item is waived on occasion). Therefore the cost to Eric of switching his mortgage to another lender is slightly higher than the cost of simply renewing with the existing lender. However, the true cost of a transfer-in is considerably less than a refinancing (which could be close to $1,000).

Heed these words of caution before embarking on a switching expedition. Institutional lenders will not allow a switch from a private lender or an individual; the transfer-out must be from another institutional lender. This is not a legal prohibition; it is just one of the conditions lenders impose. Another is the usual requirement that the property be owner-occupied, and a single family dwelling. No switching or transfer-ins on investment or income-producing property.

Switching is not possible in certain provinces of Canada (especially in Atlantic Canada). Provincial legislation there does not permit mortgage transfers to be delivered instead of discharges, effectively destroying the usefulness of switching.

Most importantly, while Eric could switch lenders for the amount currently owing, and even reduce the amount owing on a transfer-in, switching is not allowed if Eric wants to increase the size of the mortgage. If Eric owes $90,000, he can switch lenders, prepay $10,000, and sign a mortgage-amending agreement for $80,000. But if he wants to increase the mortgage to $100,000, it's back to square one refinancing the loan. In fact, a formal refinancing for $100,000 would be needed whether Eric stayed with Byebye Bank, or if he switched lenders to Welcome Trust.

Finally, keep in mind that not all institutional lenders offer a switch or transfer-in program. Some do, some don't; it depends on the individual lender. Like every other mortgage feature, shop around.

Technically, the switch or transfer-in is not one of the features making up the perfect mortgage. Instead, it is a vehicle that provides considerable flexibility to current borrowers, enabling them to acquire the perfect mortgage features when their mortgages come due. Shifting from a lender with a stale package of features to one offering many progressive items included in the perfect mortgage has never been easier or cheaper. Why reluctantly retain the status quo if you are unhappy with your current lender, especially when change is possible at nominal extra expense? In the long run, the benefits far outweigh the additional costs. All the more reason why existing homeowners can and should shop for a mortgage, seeking out the perfect mortgage even when they already have a mortgage!

When Your Mortgage Matures, You Can:

- retire the mortgage,
- renew the mortgage,
- refinance the mortgage, or,
  to get all the perfect mortgage features you want:
- take advantage of the latest alternative, the switch or "transfer-in."

21
Home Equity Loans/
Lines of Credit

Putting the equity in your home to work

In the mid-1980s some of the major institutional lenders began marketing a "new" mortgage product under a variety of different names. Behind the descriptive veneer was an old idea, repackaged under the generic title "the home equity loan." While it is not one of the perfect mortgage features in the truest sense, it's the perfect type of vehicle for those people who want to realize on the investment potential in their homes.

Over time a homeowner's equity can increase in two ways: by actively paying down the outstanding principal; and by passively benefitting from increasing property values, the so-called "new equity." To realize on this great, untapped source of potential loan business, lenders began offering the "home equity loan," where you use the equity in your home as collateral for a loan. Applied properly, this new/old idea can be an effective way of converting that equity into a source of revenue.

Today's home equity loans are markedly different from conventional mortgages. Instead of having a fixed rate of interest, it fluctuates based on a predetermined set of criteria. In other words, it's a variable-rate mortgage, just like most commercial loans.

If Bill borrowed $100,000 on a conventional mortgage, the lender would advance $100,000 to Bill in one lump sum. With a $100,000 home equity loan, that's the *maximum* amount Bill is allowed to owe. Whenever funds are needed, Bill can "draw down" on the loan. Bill can borrow as much as he wants, whenever he wants. There's no need to ever draw down the full $100,000.

With a home equity loan, there's no need for Bill to receive the full $100,000 all at one time either. The amount he owes can go up and down as he borrows money and repays the loan, just like a yo-yo. Interest is only paid on what Bill owes at any time.

These lines of credit also provide another important benefit. As a personal loan, the primary security being a promissory note, it's *fully open*. Therefore not only can Bill borrow as much as he wants, whenever he wants, Bill also can pay back as much as he wants, whenever he wants, without facing any penalties. However, as institutional lenders always want as much security as possible, a "collateral" mortgage must be registered against Bill's house, the mortgage being additional security for the loan. It's this collateral mortgage, the home equity being used as security, that helps Bill get such a good rate of interest on his line of credit.

Home equity loans resemble business loans in another way as well. Lenders can insist on having the funds repaid "on demand," whenever they want. Practically speaking, borrowers who meet their obligations on time have little to worry about. Demand loans like these can remain outstanding for years. But knowing that the funds can be called in at any time helps ensure that borrowers like Bill keep their loans up-to-date.

Today's new-style home equity loan bears an uncanny resemblance to a "revolving" line of credit, the cornerstone of commercial borrowing, typically available only to business borrowers. And that's really what the home equity line of credit is—a commercial-style loan grafted onto the residential mortgage market.

As with other perfect mortgage features, not all institutional lenders offer home equity loans. And no two line-of-credit packages are identical either. Once again, borrowers must shop around first, and compare what the competition is offering, before making any commitments.

What are some of the differences to consider?

- The type of property that is acceptable security. Some lenders limit revolving lines of credit to owner-occupied homes, while others will also allow them against investment properties.
- How much money will be advanced? Depending on the lender, anywhere from 66.6% to 75% of the appraised value of the house will be lent, less any currently outstanding mortgages. But some lenders may impose a minimum on how much can be borrowed, a maximum (regardless of the property's value), or both.

- What type of mortgage will be granted? Most institutional lenders will allow home equity loans to be second mortgages, provided the total amount of the first and second mortgages (assuming it is fully advanced) does not exceed the lending limit (66.6% to 75% of the appraised value of the house).
- What is the interest rate? Often it's a floating rate of prime plus $\frac{1}{2}$% on the amount of the loan outstanding. But some lenders charge less and others charge more. Even so, the rates on home equity loans are the lowest available, and are significantly lower than those for unsecured personal loans, because the collateral for the loan is your house. Compare that against the interest rate on many second mortgages—the first mortgage rate plus 3%.
- How much must be repaid each month? Most lenders insist that at least the interest be paid back monthly. But others require that a fixed percentage of principal also be repaid each month.
- What are the set-up costs in arranging a home equity loan? While the charges should be similar to those for conventional mortgages, they do differ from lender to lender. Expect to pay the normal appraisal/administrative fee, although it is waived occasionally. And don't forget about legal fees and disbursements either. One way to reduce the bill for legal fees is to arrange a home equity loan when you complete your home purchase or refinance an existing loan. With much of the necessary work already being done, the line of credit transaction can be completed for half its normal cost. Also, ask if there are any annual fees, service charges or "administrative" costs.

Because of the floating- or variable-interest rate, home equity loans certainly aren't for everyone. Even at the best of times, interest rates are the great uncertainty. Despite a slightly better rate than its conventional cousin, it never should be arranged just to finance the purchase of a home. Any short-term benefits could easily be lost, and the ownership of your home jeopardized, if interest rates crept upwards over the long haul.

Then what's so appealing about a home equity loan? The way it lets people gain access to the equity in their homes quickly. Most people don't have the cash to take advantage of a good investment opportunity. Borrowing money on a mortgage takes time—applying for the loan, giving the appropriate explanation where the money will be used, waiting for approval, and then having your lawyer process the deal. Because of the considerable time lag between asking for the money and actually getting it, excellent investment opportunities could be lost.

Having the foresight to arrange a home equity loan ahead of time could be the difference between landing that deal and losing it. After all, the best time to establish borrowing power is when you don't really need it. Once the collateral mortgage is registered, the line of credit automatically is in place. Until you use it, no interest is paid. And when you need the money, everything is in place and ready. All you have to do is write a cheque. There's no need to apply every time you draw against your line of credit, and no need to give any explanation of where the money is going. No longer do you have to worry about losing an investment opportunity because you don't have the money in place.

And that is where home equity loans make most sense, and have been most popular to date—when borrowed money is used to make more money—to buy income-producing property or to invest in a business. This is the one time Revenue Canada lets homeowners deduct the interest on their mortgages against other income, even where the collateral mortgage is secured against their principal residence. It's how the borrowed funds were used, rather than the security for the loan, that determines interest deductibility in Canada.

What are other investment applications for the home equity line of credit? It's an attractive alternative to a margin account for investors in the stock market. The same is true when buying property to be sold in a short period of time, or when financing the down payment for an income-producing property. But even home equity loans are no substitute for the long-term, permanent, fixed-rate debt demanded by some investments.

Home equity loans are an excellent way for homeowners to start putting the equity in their homes to work. It can be the icing on the cake why homeowners should prepay their mortgages. Home equity loans allow borrowers to get back, for investment use, both the money prepaid earlier plus the fresh equity generated by an increase in house values. Applied properly, they enable borrowers to write off the interest expense against other income they earn. Used wisely, they allow homeowners to be a little more cash-flow rich, and to capitalize on an opportunity when both the time and the investment are right.

When Shopping for the Perfect Mortgage Home Equity Loan/Line of Credit, Ask:

1) What type of property is acceptable security? principal residence only?
2) How much money will be advanced? is there a minimum? a maximum?
3) What type of mortgage will be granted? first mortgage only? second mortgage too?
4) What is the interest rate? What is it based on?
5) How much must be repaid each month? Does any principal have to be repaid?
6) What are the set-up charges in arranging a home equity loan?

22
You'd Better Shop Around

Everyone can benefit from The Perfect Mortgage

Before reading this book, a number of people were probably quite skeptical about the need to shop for a mortgage. By now, we should be preaching to the converted. Just by reading a mortgage brochure, the average Canadian will be amazed at the new concepts now available in the marketplace. Ironically, the recent explosion of different features has made the task of booking a mortgage increasingly difficult. With so much to choose from, borrowers now suffer from the excesses of abundance.

Armed with *The Perfect Mortgage*, Canadian borrowers have the necessary information to negotiate with a mortgage lender from strength. The traditional borrowers lament—"if I only knew then what I know now"—no longer applies. Whether arranging a loan to finance a purchase or to refinance an existing mortgage, borrowers can confidently shop, compare, ask and examine. Investing time today in search of the perfect mortgage will pay handsome dividends in the future.

The benefits of shopping for a mortgage are never immediate. And success will not always be measured in dollars and cents. Instead it will gauged by the flexibility a mortgage package provides, and the anxiety eliminated when circumstances change. Usually success will be measured in the negative, by the *absence* of problems. A good mortgage package will allow borrowers to do what they want, when they want, with a minimum of restrictions and fees. Poor features will tie a borrower's hands, causing grief and aggravation, not to mention extra costs. Although the perfect mortgage features will only be needed at some future, indefinite time, they must be in place *now*, before making any commitment to a loan. If they're not in the mortgage, they're not available for future use.

As we have seen, generally accepted ideas and principles are not always in the best interest of the borrower. Marketing hype can create even more confusion for borrowers. What *The Perfect Mortgage* has done is provide an objective analysis of mortgage features currently available in the marketplace. What individual borrowers now must do is decide which options are most appealing.

But *The Perfect Mortgage* has also uncovered a number of serious faults in the system, cracks that can easily become chasms into which the unsuspecting borrower can fall. Despite all the changes in the mortgage industry in recent years, there is still considerable room for improvement. Only by understanding the problems can we ever hope to implement the solutions.

Finally, *The Perfect Mortgage* lays down a challenge to the lending industry—to offer all its features in one package. While every feature and option examined in this book is currently available in the marketplace, not one lender has consolidated everything together. As was stated in Chapter 1, just because the perfect mortgage doesn't exist, doesn't mean it can't exist. When weekly mortgages were first introduced in the mid-1980s, the first lender to offer it garnered front-page headlines. It was a major news story. The next lender to follow suit barely received media coverage. But who was the ultimate victor? The Canadian borrower.

So too with the perfect mortgage. The first lender that responds to the challenge will find the response much more favourable than the second, the third or the tenth. And who will be the ultimate winner? Once again, the Canadian borrower. Until that happens, the key to success for borrowers is to familiarize yourselves with the mortgage features currently available, rank them according to your own unique needs and wants, and then seek the lender offering the greatest number of those products. Just like Mary, the borrower in the poem at the beginning of this book, you'll find it's the first step to borrowing money worry-free.

Appendix

Amortization Schedule

AMOUNT BORROWED	$100,000.00
ANNUAL INTEREST RATE	12% interest factor → 0.009758794179192
COMPOUNDED	6 months, not in advance
PAYMENT	$1,031.90 payable 12 times per year
AMORTIZATION PERIOD	25.000 years or 300.00 payments

#	date	interest	principal	balance	total interest
1	FEB 1 1989	975.88	56.02	99,943.98	975.88
2	MAR 1 1989	975.33	56.57	99,887.41	1,951.21
3	APR 1 1989	974.78	57.12	99,830.29	2,925.99
4	MAY 1 1989	974.22	57.68	99,772.61	3,900.21
5	JUN 1 1989	973.66	58.24	99,714.37	4,873.87
6	JUL 1 1989	973.09	58.81	99,655.56	5,846.96
7	AUG 1 1989	972.52	59.38	99,596.18	6,819.48
8	SEP 1 1989	971.94	59.96	99,536.22	7,791.42
9	OCT 1 1989	971.35	60.55	99,475.67	8,762.77
10	NOV 1 1989	970.76	61.14	99,414.53	9,733.53
11	DEC 1 1989	970.17	61.73	99,352.80	10,703.70
12	JAN 1 1990	969.56	62.34	99,290.46	11,673.26
13	FEB 1 1990	968.96	62.94	99,227.52	12,642.22
14	MAR 1 1990	968.34	63.56	99,163.96	13,610.56
15	APR 1 1990	967.72	64.18	99,099.78	14,578.28
16	MAY 1 1990	967.09	64.81	99,034.97	15,545.37
17	JUN 1 1990	966.46	65.44	98,969.53	16,511.83
18	JUL 1 1990	965.82	66.08	98,903.45	17,477.65
19	AUG 1 1990	965.18	66.72	98,836.73	18,442.83
20	SEP 1 1990	964.53	67.37	98,769.36	19,407.36
21	OCT 1 1990	963.87	68.03	98,701.33	20,371.23
22	NOV 1 1990	963.21	68.69	98,632.64	21,334.44
23	DEC 1 1990	962.54	69.36	98,563.28	22,296.98
24	JAN 1 1991	961.86	70.04	98,493.24	23,258.84
25	FEB 1 1991	961.18	70.72	98,422.52	24,220.02
26	MAR 1 1991	960.49	71.41	98,351.11	25,180.51
27	APR 1 1991	959.79	72.11	98,279.00	26,140.30
28	MAY 1 1991	959.08	72.82	98,206.18	27,099.38
29	JUN 1 1991	958.37	73.53	98,132.65	28,057.75
30	JUL 1 1991	957.66	74.24	98,058.41	29,015.41
31	AUG 1 1991	956.93	74.97	97,983.44	29,972.34
32	SEP 1 1991	956.20	75.70	97,907.74	30,928.54

33	OCT 1	1991	955.46	76.44	97,831.30	31,884.00
34	NOV 1	1991	954.72	77.18	97,754.12	32,838.72
35	DEC 1	1991	953.96	77.94	97,676.18	33,792.68
36	JAN 1	1992	953.20	78.70	97,597.48	34,745.88
37	FEB 1	1992	952.43	79.47	97,518.01	35,698.31
38	MAR 1	1992	951.66	80.24	97,437.77	36,649.97
39	APR 1	1992	950.88	81.02	97,356.75	37,600.85
40	MAY 1	1992	950.08	81.82	97,274.93	38,550.93
41	JUN 1	1992	949.29	82.61	97,192.32	39,500.22
42	JUL 1	1992	948.48	83.42	97,108.90	40,448.70
43	AUG 1	1992	947.67	84.23	97,024.67	41,396.37
44	SEP 1	1992	946.84	85.06	96,939.61	42,343.21
45	OCT 1	1992	946.01	85.89	96,853.72	43,289.22
46	NOV 1	1992	945.18	86.72	96,767.00	44,234.40
47	DEC 1	1992	944.33	87.57	96,679.43	45,178.73
48	JAN 1	1993	943.47	88.43	96,591.00	46,122.20
49	FEB 1	1993	942.61	89.29	96,501.71	47,064.81
50	MAR 1	1993	941.74	90.16	96,411.55	48,006.55
51	APR 1	1993	940.86	91.04	96,320.51	48,947.41
52	MAY 1	1993	939.97	91.93	96,228.58	49,887.38
53	JUN 1	1993	939.07	92.83	96,135.75	50,826.45
54	JUL 1	1993	938.17	93.73	96,042.02	51,764.62
55	AUG 1	1993	937.25	94.65	95,947.37	52,701.87
56	SEP 1	1993	936.33	95.57	95,851.80	53,638.20
57	OCT 1	1993	935.40	96.50	95,755.30	54,573.60
58	NOV 1	1993	934.46	97.44	95,657.86	55,508.06
59	DEC 1	1993	933.51	98.39	95,559.47	56,441.57
60	JAN 1	1994	932.55	99.35	95,460.12	57,374.12
120	JAN 1	1999	853.97	177.93	87,329.89	111,157.89
180	JAN 1	2004	713.26	318.64	72,769.89	158,511.89
240	JAN 1	2009	461.26	570.64	46,695.15	194,351.15
289	FEB 1	2013	113.51	918.39	10,712.81	208,931.91
290	MAR 1	2013	104.54	927.36	9,785.45	209,036.45
291	APR 1	2013	95.49	936.41	8,849.04	209,131.94
292	MAY 1	2013	86.36	945.54	7,903.50	209,218.30
293	JUN 1	2013	77.13	954.77	6,948.73	209,295.43
294	JUL 1	2013	67.81	964.09	5,984.64	209,363.24
295	AUG 1	2013	58.40	973.50	5,011.14	209,421.64
296	SEP 1	2013	48.90	983.00	4,028.14	209,470.54
297	OCT 1	2013	39.31	992.59	3,035.55	209,509.85
298	NOV 1	2013	29.62	1,002.28	2,033.27	209,539.47
299	DEC 1	2013	19.84	1,012.06	1,021.21	209,559.31
300	JAN 1	2014	9.97	1,021.21	0.00	209,569.28

last payment (payment #300) is $1,031.18.

ulations were prepared using conventional compound interest
No liability is assumed as to the interpretation or use of these